HITTING THE WALL

HITTING THE WALL

Eliminate the Beliefs That Sabotage
Your Business and Your Life

SHELLY LEFKOE & VAHAN YEPREMYAN

LIONCREST
PUBLISHING

HITTING THE WALL
Eliminate the Beliefs That Sabotage Your Business and Your Life

FIRST EDITION

ISBN   978-1-5445-4370-3 *Hardcover*
       978-1-5445-4369-7 *Paperback*
       978-1-5445-4371-0 *Ebook*

From Shelly:

To my beloved Morty—thank you for creating a process that changes people's lives and for changing mine by coming into it. I miss you every day.

To my mom and dad—thank you for loving me unconditionally every day of my life.

To Blake and Britt, my shining stars—you amaze me every day. I am so proud to be your mama.

From Vahan:

To my dear parents, Sarkis and Nona, to whom I owe all of my success—thank you for your unconditional love, never-ending support, and constant encouragement. Words cannot begin to describe my gratitude and appreciation for all you have done for me.

To my daughter, Ava—thank you for filling my life with joy and laughter. Being your dad is the best thing that has ever happened to me.

.

CONTENTS

FOREWORD

ERIC EDMEADES, FOUNDER OF THE BUSINESS FREEDOM ACADEMY AND WILDFIT®

Beliefs matter.

For instance, what you believe about this book and yourself will determine whether or not you buy this book. If you believe that the book is valuable and life-changing (it is), but you don't believe that you will apply what you learn, then you probably won't buy it.

So it is my job to help you believe in this book, to help you see that this book is valuable and life-changing and that it is so enjoyable and practical that you will read it easily and put its principles to work in your life before you have even turned the last page.

I have known both Shelly and Vahan for many years, and I can tell you that the information they have put into this book will pay you dividends. Understanding your beliefs, how they were formed, what they really are, and how they impact your life can be one of the most rewarding and powerful breakthroughs you ever experience. That is what is ahead of you on the following pages.

What we believe about the world and, for that matter, about ourselves changes how we see the world around us. Further, our beliefs also influence how we *respond* to the world around us. The challenge is that many of the beliefs we hold—some so deeply that we don't even know we hold them—were formed in a way that now limits us or, put another way, that holds us back.

Imagine a single woman desperately seeking a partner but simultaneously believing that "all the good men are married." A friend invites her to a party, but since there is no hope of meeting someone, perhaps she refuses. Or, if she goes to the party, she sees a man she finds intriguing but believes him to be married because he keeps talking to one particular woman.

Our single woman's beliefs might prevent her from attending the party at all or, if she does go, make it impossible to learn that the man she was looking at happens to be at the party with his sister, who is helping him with his dating life.

How many opportunities will she miss as long as she holds on to this belief?

When you change a belief, you change the way you see the world and you change the way you respond to the world. In other words, changing or eliminating beliefs that hold you back can change everything.

Shelly Lefkoe is both a dear friend and a pioneer; she has helped thousands of people upgrade their life experiences, and now, for the first time, her techniques and concepts are captured in a book. Don't give it another thought: this is a book that you will look back on with gratitude.

Through my company, WILDFIT, we have helped hundreds of thousands of people, in over one hundred countries, with their food psychology to help them lose weight and improve their health. Shelly's contributions to our team and members have been incredibly valuable.

Vahan is also a good friend and someone I look up to both because of his tremendous business success and his ability to see what is possible, to look past the limits, and to discover the expansive open universe of potential that exists on the other side of limiting beliefs. Once, on a trip we shared to Africa, Vahan and I sat around a fire with the Hadza people of Tanzania and discussed all manner of topics. It was a fascinating conversation that led me to hope that Vahan would, one day, share his ideas and perspectives in a book. And now he has.

Together, Shelly and Vahan have created a book that you will enjoy and, more importantly, that you will look back on as *important*. You may, well, look back at your life as *before* and *after* you read this book.

A TALE OF TWO ENTREPRENEURS

Two entrepreneurs sit in Vahan's law firm conference room, negotiating a deal. One is the owner of a high-volume gas station with a car wash, and just by looking at him, you can tell he is busy and stressed. He has two cell phones out on the table in front of him, both of which blink and buzz throughout the meeting. Each time, he dives at the phone in question and quickly types out a response or picks up the call and begins spewing out instructions, step-by-step, on everything from managerial processes to more technical troubleshooting. With each interruption, he has to backtrack to get his thoughts on the discussion at hand. He looks disheveled and agitated, yet he holds a slight smile within his expression—a certain sense of pride mixed with exhaustion.

By contrast, the other entrepreneur is calm and unruffled. He owns nine gas stations, most with car washes, located all over Southern California. He has over ten times the business of the "busy" entrepreneur—over ten times the employees, problems, responsibilities, and churn—but in the two-hour span of the meeting, he pulls out his cell phone only once, and only during a break, to read a text from his son. Both entrepreneurs have multiple employees and multiple problems to solve and decisions to make, yet only one of the two appears tense and frazzled. Why?

It all boils down to their beliefs.

The stressed-out entrepreneur holds beliefs that cause him to distrust others' ability to make good decisions. He believes statements like "If you want it done right, you have to do it yourself" and "Successful entrepreneurs must be busy and always in charge." As a result, he works nonstop in pursuit of a successful business.

In contrast, the calm, unruffled entrepreneur holds beliefs that enable him to feel confident that he can find good people and train them to do a good job. He believes people can be trusted. As a result, he delegates essential work to grow and scale his business, leaving him free to look at his phone when he chooses, like answering a text from his son during a break.

Beliefs are powerful. We form them based on personal experiences, interactions, and observations. Without even realizing it, these beliefs impact every area of our lives. They create our thoughts, feelings, and actions. They affect our relationships and overall well-being. And as entrepreneurs, they impact our business and success.

Could the stressed-out entrepreneur become more like the calm one? Yes. But not without doing some inner work to change how he sees himself, other people, and the world.

That's where this book comes in.

ELIMINATE BELIEFS, LIVE YOUR VALUES

You may not have the same beliefs as our agitated entrepreneur, but like every other human being on the planet, you probably have beliefs that hold you back in some area of your business or personal life. Do any of the following sound familiar?

- Feeling like you're not good enough, no matter how much you accomplish
- Knowing it's okay to make mistakes, but still feeling like a failure when you do
- Feeling like a fraud because you don't think you're as successful as people think you are
- Needing the approval of others to feel okay about yourself

These feelings all stem from your beliefs—statements about reality that you hold as *the* truth. These beliefs underlie behavior patterns that can keep you from achieving your goals. They can prevent you from starting a business in the first place, from scaling your company, and from enjoying a balanced life full of purpose and joy.

Some of you may be skeptical that beliefs hold this much power. In Chapter 1, we'll address this objection head-on with scientific proof that beliefs limit us. We'll also provide multiple real-life examples of how eliminating these beliefs allowed people to change behaviors and achieve goals.

Once you understand the truth that beliefs limit us, it's time to look inside yourself: What beliefs are limiting *you*? In Chapter 2, we'll walk through the process of identifying the behavior patterns that interfere with your ability to reach your goals and the beliefs that cause those patterns.

Then we're on to the Lefkoe Belief Elimination Process, the key to getting rid of the beliefs that sabotage your business and your life. In Chapter 3, we'll walk you through each step of the process, from understanding how your limiting beliefs are formed to saying farewell to those beliefs for good.

The Lefkoe Belief Elimination Process eradicates beliefs at the root, but eliminating *all* of the beliefs responsible for a behavior pattern can take some time. What can you do in the moment when a belief you haven't handled yet causes you to feel anxious or angry or stressed out? In Chapter 4, we present the Lefkoe Occurring Process—a way to manage those uncomfortable experiences in the moment until the root belief is permanently eliminated.

As you eliminate beliefs, you will find yourself set free to achieve the goals for your business, give back to your community in meaningful ways, make a difference in the lives around you, experience more joy and less stress—in short, you will be free to live a life worth living, one based on your deepest values. In Chapter 5, Vahan—an entrepreneur, just like you—shares his thoughts on adopting empowering beliefs and creating opportunities to live life to the fullest and make a difference in the world around you.

AN ENTREPRENEUR AND A SPEAKER WALK INTO A CONFERENCE...

Back in 2015, Shelly was speaking at Mindvalley's personal growth conference in Costa Rica, called A-Fest. During one of her talks, Shelly spoke about limiting beliefs and specifically the way they keep people from doing what makes sense to them and from living the life they want.

Vahan was sitting in the audience. Several years earlier, as he had begun to work on his own limiting beliefs, he'd noticed how eliminating them positively and powerfully impacted his businesses' growth and success. At the same time, he had seen a pattern in his clients, and he was pretty sure limiting beliefs were at the root. For example, in some cases, Vahan would give advice, which the client would readily agree made perfect sense and would then fail to follow through on after leaving his office. In other cases, the client would identify an excellent entrepreneurial opportunity, describe it with enthusiasm—and then fail to act.

In an effort to help his clients, Vahan looked for a proven system and methodology that made the process of identifying and eliminating limiting beliefs easier than what he was doing for himself. This search brought him to the conference in Costa Rica and specifically to this talk Shelly and her late husband Morty were giving.

After the session, Vahan wanted to learn more. He approached Shelly, and they spent hours sharing their experiences in working with entrepreneur clients and how beliefs had such a huge, yet mostly unrecognized, impact on their ability to successfully launch and grow their businesses. As these discussions continued over the next few days at A-Fest, they both recognized how valuable it would be for entrepreneurs, and for their businesses, to have access to and learn how to use this information about the Lefkoe Belief Elimination Process.

Having shared a passion of helping others, Vahan and Shelly decided to write a book incorporating Shelly's thirty years of experience helping thousands of clients identify and eliminate limiting beliefs and Vahan's twenty-five years of experience helping thousands of clients successfully launch and grow their businesses.

Vahan and Shelly spent the next seven years going through their respective case studies, putting the materials and methodology together, and writing the book you now hold.

VAHAN'S STORY

Vahan grew up in the USSR, under communist regime, where any form of entrepreneurship was illegal and punishable by law. All businesses and enterprises were owned and controlled by the government, and as a result, the country was characterized by immense scarcity.

Underlying this impoverished economy was widespread propaganda. The government owned and ran all TV channels, radio stations, and newspapers, and they fully controlled and carefully curated all the information and the news—all designed to control the narrative and hence the population. Everywhere one looked, TV programs, radio, songs, and speeches sold the same ideas: *Don't question authority. We know what's best for you. Don't stand out. Follow the herd. Trust the government. Don't question the status quo. Don't think for yourself.*

This government control and the beliefs that resulted created an environment where there was little innovation, progress, or improvement and little incentive to build or grow any business ideas. Most industries were inefficient and heavily subsidized by the state, and any growth that did happen came at the expense of people's health and life. Punishment for stepping out of line was just as harsh—millions were jailed, exiled to Siberia, or shot. Individuals had very little worth to the state; it was all about the Communist Party and their brutal system. As we know now, the whole system was rotten from within and eventually imploded and collapsed.

Vahan moved to the United States at the age of seventeen, bringing with him many of these limiting beliefs around entrepreneurship, success, individualism, and money. Very soon, he jumped into business ownership and politics—two options he didn't have in the USSR—but he had a hard time balancing the financial edge of entrepreneurship with the principles that had been drilled into him since he was young: *Follow the rules. Preserve the status quo. Money is the root of all evil. If you're making money, it's at the expense of someone else.*

Vahan thus found himself in an interesting space: one set of beliefs pushed him into entrepreneurship because he recognized the opportunity, while another held him back from fully exploring it and flourishing. His beliefs about not standing out, for example, made it challenging to brand and market himself and his legal services. His beliefs about money kept him from talking about it. As a result, he put off invoicing because asking for money somehow corrupted his desire to help his clients—as if his goodness were lost in getting paid.

Slowly, Vahan started recognizing his limiting beliefs for what they were. He realized that money was directly connected to his responsibilities as a business owner: he needed cash flow to hire employees, pay rent, and run the company. If he didn't have money, he couldn't hire the staff to help his clients. He couldn't take care of his people. Vahan realized that money itself wasn't inherently evil; it was a neutral entity that could be used for good.

With this new understanding, money and aiding the people around him stopped being at odds with each other. Instead, they conjoined. In addition, Vahan's organization started doing more charity work. In the Soviet Union, money was often used to get around the system, through the black market, but you couldn't really change the way things worked. In the United States, Vahan could use money in a more impactful way for himself and those around him.

Eliminating his beliefs around money, success, and individualism, amongst many others, enabled Vahan to establish a successful law firm that has represented thousands of entrepreneurs and ventures over the past twenty-five years. He has also earned many recognitions. In 2015, he received the Top Lawyers of California award, and for three consecutive years, he was named to the Best Attorneys of America list, which is reserved for the top 1 percent of the nation's lawyers. He was also named to *Inc. magazine*'s list of 5000 Greatest Entrepreneurs and Fastest-Growing Private Companies in America for five years straight and was named to *Entrepreneur Magazine*'s 360 Best Entrepreneurial Companies in America in 2019. Vahan's success is also enjoyed by his employees, as the *Los Angeles Business Journal* named his law firm the twenty-fifth best company to work for in Los Angeles.

More importantly, the belief work has allowed Vahan to embrace a more holistic approach to entrepreneurship, as he discusses in more detail in Chapter 5. By eliminating the beliefs that were holding him back, Vahan was set free to define success for himself and to pursue a more fulfilling life, rich with experiences and human connections that don't show up on financial reports or balance sheets.

Over the past twenty-five years of working with entrepreneurs, Vahan has seen firsthand how certain beliefs, if left unaddressed, can become major obstacles to personal and professional growth and success. He has watched entrepreneurs become overworked, overwhelmed, and burnt out because they hold beliefs like "What makes me good enough or important are my achievements" or "There is no success without constant sacrifice, hustle, and stress." Vahan has also seen how eliminating those beliefs can lead to success that benefits others, as well as the entrepreneurs themselves.

It's now his mission as an attorney and business consultant to empower and help entrepreneurs launch and grow their companies while thriving as business owners and people.

SHELLY'S STORY

Nobody ever knew Shelly was on television as a young girl, mainly because she never told anyone. From age three to age five, Shelly was one of the child stars on *Juvenile Jury*, a show in which Shelly and other "jurors" solved other children's problems (already living in her purpose!). Her mother saw the way some of Shelly's costars became spoiled brats and treated their parents badly. She didn't want her daughter to be that way, so she repeatedly told young Shelly, "Just remember, you're not special."

Even though her parents treated her as special at home, Shelly still held on to her mother's words and developed the belief that "It's not okay to be special." As a result, in her early adult years, she never let herself be the one out front, and she had a hard time tooting her own horn. Every time she was on the verge of a big success or step forward, she unconsciously sabotaged her progress.

In the 1970s, friends started telling Shelly about the Erhard Seminars Training (EST). She was intrigued by the results they were getting, so she signed up for the course. While she did get in touch with her desire to make a difference and had a powerful experience, the belief about not being special persisted.

Without a doubt, the best part about the EST training was that Shelly met her beloved Morty. They married in 1981 and had two daughters: Blake and Brittany.

When Shelly met Morty, he was a business consultant working with organizations to improve corporate culture. Like most consultants, he gave advice to the leaders in these organizations, who would agree with what they heard—and then do nothing. This happened often enough that Morty set out to understand, and hopefully address, the cause, and in 1985, he created a process that worked. Using the Lefkoe Belief Elimination Process, Morty helped thousands of employees in diverse industries change their behaviors when nothing else worked.

When Shelly watched Morty take a friend through the process for the first time, she was almost knocked off her chair. She knew in that moment what she was put on this planet to do: help people eliminate beliefs that keep them from living the authentic, joyful lives they were meant to live.

That same year, Morty took Shelly through the process, and her belief about not being special disappeared, allowing her to step into her purpose. She started speaking at high schools and then at large conferences all over the world, including A-Fest, which is where she met Vahan.

Morty and Shelly founded the Lefkoe Institute in 1985 and started working with individuals and organizations (in person in those days and now on Zoom) and conducting workshops across the country. When her girls were young, Shelly stayed home and performed the job of professional parent, taking responsibility for the emotional, spiritual, and intellectual development of her daughters. After they were both in school, Shelly took on most of the one-on-one sessions and ran the workshops, while Morty ran workshops, oversaw the business, and sometimes did one-on-one sessions to keep his finger in the pot.

Then, in 2015, Morty passed away after a valiant battle with cancer, leaving Shelly to step into the business owner role. At the time, she didn't know a balance sheet from a profit and loss statement, but by following the process she uses to help others, Shelly eliminated the beliefs that limited her and has since led the Lefkoe Institute to ongoing success.

Over the years, Shelly has had the privilege of helping thousands of clients worldwide rid themselves of a wide variety of problems—phobias, relationships that never seem to work, violence, procrastination, unwillingness to confront people, health and wellness issues, sexual dysfunction, and more—all by eliminating the underlying beliefs. Her programs have reached over 150,000 people worldwide, including entrepreneurs like Vahan.

WHAT THIS BOOK IS AND ISN'T

This book is not a guide on how to launch or run a business. In its pages, you will not learn how to build, scale, or sell your company, and you will certainly not learn how to write a business plan, how to assemble a team, or how to come up with a mission statement.

What you will learn is how to get out of your own way so that you can enjoy true success in your business and live a life worth living.

Before starting your business, you had a dream. To make this dream a reality, you probably loaded yourself up on information.

You either talked to people in the industry or attended expos or researched potential markets. Maybe you learned how to set up a business plan and how to motivate yourself during the daily grind. But we can almost guarantee that no one asked if you had control issues or problems with procrastination or if you worried about what people think of you.

And it's beliefs in those areas that can cause you to hit the wall, professionally and personally.

In the following chapters, we'll share with you why that is—and then we'll give you the tools to help you break through. Identifying behavior patterns, eliminating beliefs, dissolving meaning in the moment—these are the keys to reaching your potential, and you already have what you need to use them.

No more lack of confidence in your abilities. No more fear around collaboration or delegation. No more excessive stress or procrastination. It's time to create a relationship to your business that makes you feel successful in every sense of the word.

Let's get started.

CHAPTER 1
_____

BELIEFS LIMIT US

Though she worked full-time as a nurse, Carrie[1] dreamed of opening her own yoga studio. She went through the certification process and found out what kind of insurance she needed. She even found a building to lease in a conveniently located strip mall and started doing private lessons on the side.

Despite doing all of the legwork, being passionate about yoga, and having existing clients, Carrie didn't follow her dream. She was held back by the beliefs "Being an entrepreneur is too risky" and "Real security comes from having a job."

Many years ago, one of Shelly's clients called, upset that he had missed his nine-year-old daughter's soccer game—again. "I didn't want to work all weekend," Ron said. "I keep promising my kids, but I keep missing their games and their plays. My

_____

[1]   While all examples involve real individuals, some names have been changed.

wife is ready to divorce me. I'm worth $10 million. I'm on the cover of business publications. When is it going to be enough?"

Even though Ron wanted to be at his daughter's game, his beliefs—"You have to work hard to be successful" and "What makes me important are my achievements"—kept him in his office all weekend instead of at the soccer field.

Carmine began an online business with an idea that was brand new in the market. For eight months, Carmine spent all of his time perfecting his website while simultaneously pushing back the launch. In the meantime, so many competitors entered the market that his business model no longer made sense. Carmine had spent the money, he had built the website, and he had the product. But now he had no market.

For months, he had questioned himself, held back by beliefs such as "The way to be good enough is to do things perfectly" and "Mistakes and failures are bad." Eventually, those beliefs resulted in him missing his opportunity.

What do these three stories have in common? All three entrepreneurs were limited by their beliefs. They couldn't take an action they valued—something important, something they really wanted to do—because certain beliefs were holding them back. Even though they wanted to change a behavior, they didn't follow through. Why?

People think the formula for change is

$$information + motivation = change$$

You read the book, attend the workshop, start following fitness gurus on social media (in other words, you get information). You post photos and tell everyone what you learned. You are pumped, jazzed, and amped about the possibilities that lay before you (you have the motivation).

But three weeks later you've stopped going to the gym. Your workshop notes are stuffed in the back of a drawer. And there's no change.

That's because information plus motivation rarely equals change. There's another part to the equation: beliefs.

$$information + motivation - beliefs = change$$

Notice that last part? We are subtracting beliefs. No matter how much *information* you have and how *motivated* you are to change, you could have certain beliefs blocking the way. Until you "subtract" them from the equation, you and your business will likely keep hitting the wall.

SCIENTIFIC PROOF

You've no doubt heard of or read self-help books that claim to identify what really holds us back, along with solutions to overcome those roadblocks. And you might see the book in your hands as just one more voice claiming to have the answer. Before we go any further, let's dive into some scientific proof that limiting beliefs are the true obstacle to success.

RAISING STUDENT ACHIEVEMENT

Psychologists have studied this topic of beliefs for decades. Thirty years ago, Stanford's Carol Dweck looked at students who encountered more difficult classes in middle school and struggled to get the same good grades they had received in elementary school. She found that when challenged, some students gave up and decreased their efforts rather than trying harder.

Why?

They believed that their abilities were fixed and that no amount of effort could change that. In their minds, the fact that they performed poorly proved they weren't very bright, so after just one or two "failures," they lost confidence and stopped trying, which only caused their grades to plummet further.

How do we know for sure that beliefs are what stopped these students? Maybe they were just unmotivated. Or maybe they really weren't very smart after all. In elementary school, these students had worked hard and had received good grades, so neither of those explanations rings true. Ruling out laziness or low intelligence still doesn't prove that beliefs were holding them back, so Dweck and a team of researchers designed a study to test their theory.

They enrolled two groups of middle school kids into a study skills workshop of eight sessions. One group was only taught study skills. The other group was taught study skills plus the belief that they could improve their ability to learn.

Before the end of eight weeks, it became clear that some pupils had changed. Without knowing which students took the workshops that included work on their beliefs, many teachers reported that students were working harder and valuing improvement, saying things like this:

> M. was far below grade level. During the past several weeks, she has voluntarily asked for extra help from me during her lunch period in order to improve her test-taking performance. Her grades drastically improved from failing to an 84 on the most recent exam.

> J., who never puts in any extra effort and often doesn't turn in the homework on time, actually stayed up late working for hours to finish an assignment early so I could review it and give him a chance to revise it. He earned a B+ on the assignment (he had been getting C's and lower).[2]

These teachers' reports are telling, but what happened to the students' grades? The difference was quite clear: those who changed their beliefs showed an improvement in grades; those who only learned study skills did not.

Dweck's study shows that learning new study skills was not enough to improve academic performance. The key ingredient was changing the ineffective belief to a more effective one. When their beliefs changed, so did their behavior and performance.

STOPPING FELONS FROM RETURNING TO PRISON

Of course, kids are young and impressionable. Often, lessons

---

2   Carol Dweck, *Mindset: The New Psychology of Success* (New York: Ballantine Books, 2013), 14.

learned in our early years can change the direction of our entire lives. Would a change in beliefs have the same impact on adults who may already be set in their ways? Or on adults in situations where few succeed at making a lasting change?

Let's consider convicted felons.

In May 2018, the US Department of Justice released a report on state prisoner recidivism. Researchers had followed a sample of 412,731 prisoners released by thirty states in 2005. They found that nearly 68 percent of those released were arrested again within three years, 79 percent within six years, and 83 percent within nine years. Many of these arrests eventually led to prison terms. Despite their complete loss of freedom and other negative consequences associated with their actions, many still failed to change.

Some might say that convicted felons are lost causes who don't want to improve themselves or that other factors like employment discrimination against people with criminal records or lack of career skills make it harder for an ex-con to make good in the world. However, they often overlook one factor that could make a difference: their beliefs.

Can convicted felons change their beliefs in the same way children in Dweck's study did? And if so, would this change their behavior?

Shelly's late husband, Morty, decided to find out. In 1994, the Lefkoes partnered with Dr. Lee Sechrest, of the University of Arizona, to test the same process with inmates who were soon to be released back into the world.

The participants were sixteen convicts from Maplestreet House and Long Lane School, both in Connecticut, not too far from where Morty and Shelly lived at the time. Morty conducted thirteen sessions with eight of the inmates, while the other eight were part of a control group and didn't receive one-on-one work.

Before they joined the study, all sixteen participants filled out pre-measures that looked at self-esteem in various ways. Later, they were all sent post-measures. Each inmate also participated in an exit interview with an independent psychologist. After the data was collected and organized, Morty and Shelly received a report, along with comments from participants.

Without exception, every participant in the group Morty worked with eliminated or changed dozens of beliefs, at least one per session. The control group, on the other hand, did not. In addition, the change in beliefs from the first group resulted in changed behavior, as shown in comments the participants submitted:

Last weekend I went home and was with my buddies. They all carry guns and I felt like going home to get mine. Normally I would have gone and gotten it. Instead I just left. I had gone with them deliberately just to see what I would do. In the future I don't plan to hang out with these guys anymore.

I no longer "rank" on my little brother when I go home. Now I feel like I'm getting healthy. I'm going back to school and getting a high school diploma. I can get somewhere...I don't even think about selling drugs anymore.

I'm not straining like I used to. I'm not self-destructive anymore. It doesn't feel like I have to bite the bullet. My life used to be very strange, scary. I was afraid life would be a bore. I needed drugs to keep life from being boring. Always lived for the moment. None of this is true anymore.

I had thought about a career in drug and alcohol abuse counseling, but I liked easy money so I stayed selling drugs and never pursued it. I never thought about the possible consequences of selling drugs: getting killed, prison, etc. Before there was no worry, no fear. Now I am aware of what I have to lose if I go back to negative ways of thinking and acting. I used to solve all my problems with "F--- it!" Now money is not the greatest issue, happiness is.

Do these changes last? you may wonder. One of the participants, Chris, had been in jail for shooting someone over a five-dollar bill. Soon after his release, Morty and Shelly invited him to dinner. As Shelly watched him play with her daughter, she marveled at how gentle he was. "How can someone who shot people be so soft-spoken and gentle?" Shelly asked him.

"When I was young, my father told me that if anyone gets in your face and razzes you and you don't shoot them, you'll lose respect in the hood," Chris replied. "I felt like I didn't have a choice."

Soon after that, Chris visited his dad in prison and told him about the belief he had eliminated. With tears in his eyes, his dad said, "Son, I was wrong; it's not worth it."

Another participant named Jameel was a wife beater. When Morty started working with him, Jameel said, "I don't want to hit women. It just keeps happening."

During childhood, Jameel had developed the beliefs that "When you do something bad, you deserve to be punished" and "The way to punish someone is to beat them." When Jameel got rid of these beliefs, he said, "It never occurred to me that there were other ways to deal with problems."

When Morty and Shelly checked up on Jameel months later, he said he never thinks of hitting women anymore. He was enrolled in a communication course at the local community college.

Morty and Shelly's work with convicted felons shows that even people who grew up in difficult environments, picked up harmful beliefs, and engaged in destructive behavior can change their actions once they change their beliefs.

REDUCING FEAR OF PUBLIC SPEAKING

The participants in the first two studies had one thing in common: they were all underperforming in some way. The middle school students were getting poor grades, while the convicted felons were not living by society's accepted rules.

Do beliefs ever limit high achievers? And if so, does changing beliefs make a difference in their behavior?

Independent researchers attempted to answer those questions by looking at people who had a fear of public speaking. They identified potential participants who spoke weekly at Toastmasters meetings. Each person rated their fear on a scale of 1 to 10, with 10 being extreme fear. Only those with a rating of 7 or above were included in the study.

In the end, they had a group of thirty-six participants, all of whom had the same ten to fourteen beliefs underlying their fear of public speaking, such as "I'm not good enough" and "I'm not important." "People aren't interested in what I have to say." Eighteen of these people had one-on-one sessions to work on these beliefs using Morty and Shelly's process, while the others were put on a waiting list. After an average of 3.3 one-hour sessions, participants who worked on their beliefs said their fear of public speaking dropped from an average of 7 to an average of 1.5. The second group eventually had the same one-on-one sessions to work on their beliefs, but in the waiting period before they did, they experienced no improvement, despite attending Toastmasters meetings regularly.

Six months later, researchers followed up and found that participants who received one-on-one work rated their fear at an average of 2.2, just a fraction above what it had been when they finished their sessions. The lead researcher on the study said, "We had expected that the fear would come back but it didn't. They had, in fact, changed. Their fear of public speaking was gone."

This study was published in the journal *Clinical Psychology and Psychotherapy* in 2006. Since then, the Lefkoe Institute has helped more than four thousand people change their limiting beliefs around public speaking. Ordinary people *can* change their beliefs and make big changes in their lives as a result.

Frumi Barr is one of these people. Before she eliminated the beliefs that led her to fear public speaking, she had a fight-or-flight reaction every time she had to speak. "I used to be so afraid to speak that my stomach was queasy, my scalp would prickle with fear, I'd feel my temperature rising, and my voice sounded really shaky to me," she told Morty and Shelly. "All I could think of was my fear and panic. My fear of public speaking also stopped me from completing my PhD because I knew that after my book was written I would have to speak publicly in order to spread my message."

After her last session with Morty, Frumi wrote him the following email:

Dear Morty,

Last night I gave a three-hour class at Cal State Long Beach and felt no fear at all.

I can hardly believe it. As you know I was totally skeptical but as I got in front of the room and noticed no panic, my skepticism vanished.

Now I feel ready to write and promote my book that I've been procrastinating on for about a year.

I really appreciate the work you did with me. My fear is gone!

Frumi Barr

Just two years later, Frumi published her book *Confessions of a Resilient Entrepreneur: Persevering to Success*. She has since built a successful business helping executives overcome their challenges, and she's even written a second book with a foreword by Simon Sinek.

BELIEFS LIMIT OUR SUCCESS AS ENTREPRENEURS

After reading about the preceding studies, you might be convinced that beliefs limit us but wonder whether we really need a process to eliminate those beliefs and change our behavior. Once we're aware of those beliefs, can't we simply think ourselves out of them?

Here's one example of what it's like to run up against a limiting belief without a clear method to change it.

Vahan had a client—let's call him Steven—who owned valuable intellectual property that he had developed over a decade and was successfully using in his current business. A group of investors realized they could use Steven's knowledge to reach other markets and approached him with a deal to license his work and translate it outside the United States.

But Steven was skeptical. He thought something must be fishy about the deal. Vahan did his due diligence and confirmed that these were legitimate investors with a proven track record. Vahan even negotiated a licensing deal that was very favorable to his client and included a large up-front payment and a generous monthly licensing fee. But Steven continued to resist.

"How can they just hand me all this money?" Steven asked Vahan during one conversation.

"What do you mean?" Vahan asked.

"They're just going to give me all this money, and I don't have to do *anything*? They're gonna do all the hard work and just send me money every month? It doesn't add up. Something is off. People don't just give away money. You have to earn it."

Clearly, Steven had beliefs about money that kept him from moving forward with the deal. One of them was "Money doesn't grow on trees." Another was "There's no such thing as a free lunch; earning money involves hard work, struggle, sacrifice, and suffering." These beliefs drove Steven so completely that he worked himself ragged and developed serious health issues that ultimately required hospitalization.

Vahan tried to convince his client with rational arguments, for example, "You're not the one taking the easy road. The investors are the ones taking a shortcut to success. After all, it's far easier to write a check than to expend the blood, sweat, and tears you did in developing and building your intellectual property over ten years." Still, Steven wouldn't pull the trigger on the deal. When a belief stands in our way like this, we can struggle to move forward, even if everyone tells us the next step makes sense.

The investors were getting ready to move on, but before they did, Vahan convinced them to cut a check to Steven and give him a few more days to make his decision.

After the investors did so, Vahan handed the check to Steven. "Don't deposit this," Vahan said. "Take it home over the weekend. Think long and hard about it. And then, on Monday, if you still don't want it, we'll give it back, and they'll go on their way. Otherwise, we'll sign the contract, and you'll keep the check."

Over the weekend, something changed. With the check in his hand, Steven began to believe that he could have this money, that he had earned it, that he did deserve it. By Sunday night, he called Vahan and said, "I'm not giving this check back. Let's sign that contract."

Almost overnight, Steven went from being a struggling business owner to having a formidable brand now licensing his intellectual property all over the United States and the world—earning more from his licensing deals than he does from his "regular" business. All of this was possible because he changed his beliefs.

For Steven, however, it took months of conversation and a signed check in hand for him to overcome his belief that you can only earn money through hard work and suffering. Eliminating beliefs doesn't have to take that long. As we'll show you in the coming chapters, it can happen in as little as thirty minutes.

CHANGE YOUR BELIEFS, CHANGE YOUR BUSINESS—AND YOUR LIFE

Vahan had a client who owned a cosmetics line. Alexandra's unique, high-quality products had earned her many celebrity endorsements, and soon, with all of the opportunities and exposure, her business reached a turning point. To meet the demand and fulfill the high volume of purchase orders coming in, she needed additional funding for manufacturing. Not being able to secure a bank loan, Alexandra began to consider raising funds through investors.

She entered into several rounds of discussions with potential investors, including an opportunity to feature her products on the popular TV show *Shark Tank*, where business owners pitch to a group of potential investors. If interested in the product and the company, some of these high-profile investors would invest in her company in exchange for certain equity. Alexandra would also benefit from their experience, expertise, and connections.

However, there was a problem. Alexandra had some unconscious limiting beliefs around partnerships. Because of a past experience, she had concluded that she could not trust a partner, that partners tend to act in their own self-interest, taking advantage of situations. Alexandra felt that it would be unsafe and ill-advised to work with any partner and that partnerships eventually end up in disagreements, conflict, and breakup, taking down the company. She had even memorized several feuds that resulted in partnership splits, as proof of her belief.

As a result, Alexandra walked away from numerous interested investors, including some from *Shark Tank*, which would have showcased her brand on national TV and would have brought in the needed capital, network, and expertise—all because of a persistent belief that she couldn't trust anybody but herself.

Alexandra had the opportunity to launch her business to new heights, but beliefs kept her chained to the launchpad. The same happens to many entrepreneurs, often more than once. Despite their desire and preparation, they keep hitting the wall in the same places, over and over. Sometimes they get stuck before they even get off the launchpad. Other times they take off but sputter out afterward.

When either scenario occurs, entrepreneurs often look to external actions they can take to increase sales or scale their business. They look at employee performance or how the company fares against the competition.

These are all important elements to consider, but if you do so without unhooking the chains of your limiting beliefs, you will remain stuck, unable to reach the heights you have the potential to attain.

Are you ready to break free from those chains—the beliefs that create internal resistance and keep you from moving forward? The first step is finding the beliefs that stand in your way.

EXERCISE

To begin experiencing what beliefs you hold and how they impact your life, try this thought experiment:

- In this chapter, we highlighted several beliefs that were holding entrepreneurs back:
  - "Money doesn't grow on trees."
  - "There's no such thing as a free lunch; earning money involves hard work and suffering."
  - "The way to be good enough is to do things perfectly."
  - "What makes me good enough is working hard."
  - "What makes me good enough are my achievements."
  - "Being an entrepreneur is dangerous."
  - "Real security comes from having a job."
- Does this list give you a sense of what beliefs might be holding you back? Write down any beliefs that come to mind. Later, we'll show you a more systematic way to find limiting beliefs, but this is a good start.

You'll find similar exercises at the end of each chapter. We understand that some of you would rather read the book all the way through without pausing to complete them. If that's you, just make sure to come back and do them. These exercises provide the practical steps to start identifying and eliminating the beliefs that are keeping you from finding success in business and in life.

CHAPTER 2

FINDING THE BELIEFS THAT LIMIT US

A child sat at the kitchen table holding two apples. Her mother walked in and noticed the red, shiny fruit.

"Those look delicious!" the mother said. "May I have one?"

Without a word, the child took a bite out of the one in her left hand and chewed it slowly. After she'd swallowed, she lifted her right hand to her mouth and took a bite out of the second apple, again chewing slowly, almost thoughtfully.

The mom couldn't believe it. *She is so selfish!* she thought. Just as she opened her mouth to scold her daughter, the little girl held out her left hand and said, "This apple is sweeter, Mommy."

Clearly, there was a mismatch between the mother's judgment of her daughter's behavior and what her child really intended.

Similarly, there's often a mismatch between our goals and our behavior—between what we want to do and what we actually end up doing. We intend to do something, then find we don't do all we can to reach our goal. Or we intend to stop doing something only to fall back into old habits. To correct the discrepancy between what we say we want and what we actually do, we must first find the underlying reason for our actions. It doesn't help to judge ourselves for having issues. Instead, we need to look for the real culprits in our way—our limiting beliefs. In this chapter, we explain the exact steps that help you find them.

SET A GOAL

As an entrepreneur, you probably live by goal setting and achieving. Think about the goals you've recently set for yourself and your business. Maybe you've decided that you need to write a book to take your business to the next level or you need to expand your reach by doing some public speaking. Or maybe you're nearing burnout and have decided you'll be healthier and happier if you cut back your working hours.

Have you repeatedly failed to reach one or more of those goals despite having desire, despite having good intentions, and despite knowing it's the thing that will take your business to the next level?

Remember the equation presented in Chapter 1:

$$\text{information} + \text{motivation} - \text{beliefs} = \text{change}$$

If you're not making a change despite the information and motivation to do so, it's because you have beliefs stopping you. You need to dig beneath the goal to figure out the interfering pattern and the beliefs causing it.

UNCOVER THE INTERFERING PATTERN

In short, an interfering pattern is a set of behaviors that interferes with your ability to reach a goal. For example, you might want to grow your business and know that cold calling is one sure way to do that. But still you don't make the cold calls. Or you might want to keep your employees motivated and engaged, but you consistently talk down to people after they make mistakes, which effectively undercuts their motivation and engagement. In both cases, your behaviors, or interfering patterns, are preventing you from reaching your goal.

Here's another example: Tom was an aspiring day trader. By his late thirties, he'd taken a variety of courses on day trading and excelled in paper trading scenarios. He would spend all day watching the market, closely monitoring select stocks and determining exactly when to jump in and when to jump out. In a real-world application, these moves would have won him around $12,000 or more in a day.

After seeing considerable success with paper trading and practice drills, Tom was certain he had the skills to become a successful day trader. However, whenever he set out to transition from paper to real trading, he would lock up, telling himself he'd make the transition tomorrow instead—but every time tomorrow rolled around, he would falter the same as he had the day before.

Tom had a goal—become a successful day trader—but certain behavior patterns kept interfering with his progress. Even though he did well in practice trading and saw how much money he could potentially make, he hesitated. Instead of investing with real money, he stuck with paper trades, missing out on thousands of dollars in the process.

Tom's inaction is an example of an *avoidance behavior pattern*: not doing what we need to do despite our desire to do it. On the other end of the spectrum are *compulsive behavior patterns*: repeatedly engaging in certain behaviors, despite our desire to stop, because in some way we receive an emotional payoff by continuing.

Perhaps you want to write a book, but every time you sit down to write, you get distracted with social media or checking emails. Maybe you want to improve your public speaking skills, but you repeatedly put off the tasks required to prepare your presentation. Both of these are avoidance patterns.

On the other hand, perhaps you want to reduce your working hours to spend more time with your kids, but you keep overcommitting and missing family functions. Or maybe you're about to launch a new product, but you keep tweaking and tweaking and finding ways to make it better long after you could have released it. Those are compulsive patterns. Nearly every interfering behavior pattern boils down to either avoidance or compulsion.

Here's a brief list of common behavior patterns that keep entrepreneurs from reaching their goals:

Avoidance

- Putting off "difficult" conversations
- Resistance to discussing fees or invoicing

- Neglecting to delegate
- Not saying things people won't like or not giving negative feedback
- Not asking questions
- Not asking for the terms you want in a business transaction
- Staying out of situations where you would promote yourself—networking events, podcasting, and so on
- Not scheduling a speech, not asking for or being open to getting feedback on a presentation, putting off preparing your talking points
- Not making cold calls

Compulsion

- Impulsive spending
- Taking on too much work in an effort to please
- Repeatedly bragging about your successes
- Doing tasks yourself instead of delegating to others
- Spending excessive time to make a task "perfect"

It is also important to note that interfering behaviors have an emotion attached to them. In other words, your actions result from an effort to dodge or embrace a certain emotion. With avoidance behaviors, you need to figure out what emotion you are avoiding; with compulsive behaviors, you need to figure out what positive emotion you're getting out of your action. Identifying the attached emotion will help you identify the underlying belief, and identifying the belief is the first step in eliminating it.

DISCOVER THE BELIEFS THAT CAUSE THE PATTERN

By this point, you probably have an idea of some of the behavior patterns you engage in. Pick one of those behaviors and do a little thought-discovery experiment:

1. Picture yourself engaging in that behavior.
2. Notice the thoughts and feelings that emerge as you do so, and write them down.

Understanding these thoughts and feelings is very helpful in identifying the underlying belief that is causing the behavior pattern. The beliefs that limit us are innumerable, but they generally fall into four main categories:

- **Self-beliefs:** "I am [adjective]" or "I am not [adjective]." Examples: "I am incapable." "I am not good enough."
- **Topical beliefs:** "[Topic] is [adjective]." Examples: "Politicians are liars." "Relationships don't work."
- **If-then beliefs:** "If X happens, then Y will happen." Examples: "If I fail, then I'll be rejected." "If I take risks, then I'll lose everything."
- **Survival strategy beliefs:** "The way to be [adjective] is [behavior/result]" or "What makes me [adjective] is [behavior/result]." Examples: "The way to be good enough is to achieve." "What makes me worthwhile is doing things perfectly."

Understanding these categories and filling in the blanks related to our behavior patterns can help us see the limiting beliefs that are interfering with our goals. For example, if we avoid a task out of *fear*, our beliefs would revolve around our ability or the consequences of failure. If we avoid a task out of resentment, we might have beliefs about powerlessness or needing to please others.

Let's go back to Tom, our aspiring day trader. His behavior patterns came from a place of avoidance because he feared failure.

What were the beliefs behind this pattern?

To figure that out, Tom had to ask himself what he believed about failure that caused him to avoid it. He also had to ask himself what he believed would happen if he failed. In the end, Tom determined that he actually had a few underlying beliefs:

- "Mistakes and failure are bad." (topical belief)
- "If I fail, then I'm a failure." (if-then belief)
- "What makes me good enough is doing things perfectly." (survival strategy belief)

You may have a different interfering behavior pattern, but the process is the same. For example, if you avoid managing your finances, ask yourself what you believe about money that has caused this avoidance behavior. If you feel compelled to do things perfectly, ask yourself, "What positive feelings about myself do I receive when I do something perfectly?" (e.g., "I'm good enough," "I'm important," "I'm worthwhile") or "What negative feelings do I have when I don't do something perfectly?" (e.g., "I'm not good enough," "I'm not important," "I'm not worthwhile").

You may know intellectually that these beliefs are silly, but you still hold them. Shelly worked with five people who held PhDs from Harvard, yet they still held the belief "I am stupid." They attended Harvard; they graduated; they knew they weren't stupid—yet they still believed it. Shelly could have written a book about how mistakes and failures are learning opportunities—yet she still held the belief that mistakes and failures are bad.

One helpful hint: be patient with yourself when you first start this process. It will probably take some work to identify the behavior patterns standing in your way, the thoughts and feelings that come up when you engage in those behaviors, and ultimately, the beliefs that are causing those patterns.

HOW TO UNCOVER AND DISCOVER

Let's put these three ideas together to find the beliefs that are limiting you.

1. SET A GOAL

Identify something you've been unsuccessfully trying to achieve. Choose one for which your own behavior has been getting in the way.

2. UNCOVER THE INTERFERING PATTERN

Using the goal you've identified, take the following steps:

1. List the behaviors that have been getting in the way of you achieving that goal. They will show up as things you are avoiding or things you do that interfere with goal progress.
2. Choose one behavior to focus on first.
3. Identify the feelings that drive that behavior. With avoidance behaviors, notice the feeling that comes *before* you the behavior you avoid. With compulsive behaviors, notice the positive feeling that comes *after*.

3. DISCOVER THE UNDERLYING BELIEF

Using the behavior identified above, take the following steps:

1. Imagine engaging in that behavior. Notice the thoughts and feelings that emerge as you do so, and write them down.
2. Using those thoughts and feelings, try to identify which type of belief is lying underneath and use the sentence stems to help you verbalize the belief:
   A. **Self-belief:** "I am [adjective]" or "I am not [adjective]" ("I am not smart." "I don't have what it takes.")
   B. **Topical belief:** "[Topic] is [adjective]." ("Money is scarce." "Lawyers are not trustworthy.")
   C. **If-then belief:** "If X happens, then Y will happen." ("If I don't meet expectations, then I'll be rejected." "If I disagree with others, then I'll be disliked.")
   D. **Survival strategy belief:** "The way to be [adjective] is [behavior/result]" or "What makes me [adjective] is [behavior/result]." ("The way to be good enough is by achieving." "What makes me important is standing out.")

Here's a real-life example taken from a session in which one of the Lefkoe Institute facilitators took a client named Brian through the process of finding the beliefs that were limiting him.

Set a goal: Have a better relationship with my wife and business partner.

Uncover the interfering pattern:

> *Facilitator:* "Brian, what's an emotion or behavior you want to change?"

Brian: "I'm too critical sometimes. I'll get mad and say things that are hurtful."

Facilitator: "What kinds of things get you angry and have you get critical?"

Brian: "When someone doesn't do what they're supposed to do, especially if they're already supposed to know what to do."

Facilitator: "Got it. And what's an example of that?"

Brian: "I have a business partner, and he met with a client, and he quoted the price wrong. Then I had to fix it and have an unhappy customer."

Facilitator: "And what did you do next?"

Brian: "I was like, 'What were you thinking? Were you *even* thinking? We've gone over this before. Any reasonable person would have known not to do it that way.' I went on for a bit. I kind of chewed him out."

Facilitator: "It sounds like you were really mad."

Brian: "Yeah, I was."

Facilitator: "And is this typical of what happens?"

Brian: "Oh yeah. You can ask my girlfriend. She'll tell you I do that to her too, unfortunately."

Facilitator: "Got it. So it doesn't just affect you in your business but in your personal life."

Brian: "Unfortunately."

Discover the underlying belief:

Facilitator: "So what do you believe that has you get angry when someone doesn't do what you expect them to do?"

Brian: "I have no idea."

Facilitator: "That's okay. Most people have no idea what they believe that causes them to have the feelings and behavior they have. So I'll ask you a few questions that can help us figure this out."

Brian: "Alright."

Facilitator: "So I want you to imagine a situation in the future where your business partner or someone else is given a task, but they mess up some details that they should know how to do well. Let me know when you've got that in your mind."

Brian: "I've got it."

Facilitator: "Now, as you imagine that, do you feel some anger?"

Brian: "Yes."

Facilitator: "Okay. And as you notice the anger, also notice some of the thoughts that might be fueling the anger."

Brian: "Okay."

Facilitator: "I'll pause for a bit to let the thoughts simmer."

[Pause]

Brian: "So what comes up is terrible. I almost don't want to admit it. But I think they're incompetent."

Facilitator: "I see."

Brian: "Yeah, and that I'll have to fix the mess they created."

Facilitator: "Okay. That makes sense. So you have thoughts that they're incompetent and you have to fix the mess they created."

Brian: "Yeah."

Facilitator: "Okay. One thing that can help us translate your thoughts into a belief statement is if you do a sentence completion exercise with me. Would you like to try that?"

Brian: "Sure."

Facilitator: "Okay. Try completing this sentence: 'If they screw up, it means…'"

Brian: "If they screw up, it means…that they're incompetent. If they screw up, it means…I'll have to do it myself… But I'm starting to think it's not about them screwing up. I feel it's really about not getting the end results."

Facilitator: "Try doing the exercise starting with 'If they don't get the end results…'"

Brian: "If they don't get the end results, I'll have to do it myself... Yeah. That feels true."

Facilitator: "Got it."

Brian: "But something feels like it's missing. It feels like this is really about me, not them."

Facilitator: "Oh."

Brian: "Yeah, like it says something about me when we don't get the results we're supposed to get."

Facilitator: "And what does that say about you?"

Brian: "It says that I'm incompetent."

Facilitator: "I see. I'd like you to try saying those words out loud: 'I'm incompetent.' And notice how it feels to say that."

Brian: "I'm incompetent. Ugh. It feels awful."

Facilitator: "And, of course, you know that statement isn't the truth about you, but does it feel true on a gut level even though you know it's not true?"

Brian: "Yeah, I do know that it's not true really. But, yes, it does feel true."

Facilitator: "And this belief, 'I'm incompetent,' would it explain why you feel angry when your colleague or girlfriend doesn't get desired results?"

Brian: "Well, a bit. And here's what I just noticed: I'm only getting mad when I gave the instructions and they weren't followed. It's all things where I told them what I wanted and they still didn't do it. That's why I feel incompetent. It's like I'm mad at them for making me feel like I did a poor job instructing them."

Facilitator: "Got it. That's an amazing insight."

One thing you may notice about this dialogue with Brian is that his first thoughts didn't seem to explain his feelings. His own instincts told him he needed to go deeper. The same may happen to you. When you uncover your thoughts and emotions, you may not always find the underlying belief the first time. That's okay. If you persist, eventually, like Brian, you will find a belief that seems to truly explain your feelings and behavior.

BE THE CHANGE

To achieve our full potential as entrepreneurs and as human beings, we need to know how to find out where we want to go (our goals), what's in the way (our behaviors), and the root causes of what's in our way (our beliefs).

As long as the beliefs remain in place, we will struggle to make changes that will allow our businesses to grow and that will make our lives truly worth living.

In the next chapters, we'll discover how to take one belief holding you back and dismantle it. You'll then increase your freedom to take actions that may seem difficult or impossible today.

EXERCISE

Now it's time for you to go through the process yourself:

1. **Set a goal.** Choose one for which your own behavior has been getting in the way.

2. **Uncover the interfering pattern.** Identify the feelings that drive that behavior, whether they are negative feelings that come before (avoidance) or positive feelings you have after (compulsion).

3. **Discover the underlying belief.** Using those thoughts and feelings, try to identify which type of belief is lying underneath. Fill in the blanks of the belief statements given earlier.

After you discover the belief, you're ready to eliminate it.

CHAPTER 3

ELIMINATING THE BELIEFS THAT LIMIT US

When Orville and Wilbur Wright flew the first airplane at Kitty Hawk, North Carolina, observers were amazed at what they saw. For years, many had created planes and gliders that failed, some rather publicly and spectacularly. People even made humorous films that showcased these unsuccessful flying contraptions.

Having heard about these failures and seen movies about the botched flights, many people believed that no one would ever make a machine that could fly. Then, in 1903, the Wright brothers succeeded.

What happened to the beliefs of those skeptics? They vanished in an instant.

Of course, when we have a belief about physical reality, simply seeing the evidence for ourselves can lead to change. But when our belief is an abstraction, such as "I'm not good enough" or "Failure is bad," change is not so easy.

Fortunately, Morty Lefkoe figured out a way to overcome this difficulty. In this chapter, we provide a time-tested approach to eliminating these hard-to-change beliefs. Other approaches teach you how to cope with your personal limitations. We're going to show you how to get rid of the beliefs so there's nothing to cope with.

THE LEFKOE BELIEF ELIMINATION PROCESS

In Chapter 1, we showed how Morty helped numerous people with a fear of public speaking eliminate beliefs and greatly reduce or eliminate their fear. We're now going to walk you through the process he used and that the Lefkoe Institute still uses today.

You did the prep work for this process in the previous chapter when you identified beliefs that are keeping you from reaching your goals. As you continue reading, focus on one of the beliefs you previously identified, the one that seems to be at the root of many of your struggles.

It's important to go through the following steps one at a time in order. Here's a quick overview before we dive into each step in detail:

- Step 1: The source
- Step 2: Alternative interpretations
- Step 3: No seeing
- Step 4: No meaning
- Step 5: Kinesthetic/feeling
- Step 6: Check the belief

If you would like to be guided through the process of eliminating a belief before you go through the steps that follow, check out http://hittingthewall.net. If you're ready to dive into the steps on your own, keep reading.

STEP 1: THE SOURCE
Where did this belief come from?

When we come into this world, we know nothing about the way things work. We don't know if we're good enough or not, capable or not, or important or not. We don't know whether life is hard or easy. We don't know whether money is abundant or scarce, or if people are reliable or untrustworthy.

Because we don't know how things work, as young children we constantly ask why, much to our parents' dismay: Why is the sky blue? Why can't I stay up late? Why can't I have ice cream for dinner?

We also ask why in our attempt to make sense of what we experience, observe, and hear. As we watch our parents struggle with money, for example, we ask ourselves why and then come up with our own conclusions, like "Money is scarce." If we feel like we can't live up to our parents' expectations and ask ourselves why, we might conclude, "I'm not good enough." If we observe our parents being fearful and hear them frequently tell us to be careful, we might conclude "The world is a dangerous place." In this way, we form beliefs about ourselves, others, and how the world works.

After you identify the belief underlying your pattern, ask yourself,

"Where did this belief come from?" The circumstances or origins you identify are called "the source."

In general, the source of a belief can be found in one of three places:

- **Personal experiences:** Things that happened to you personally, whether in childhood or as an adult. Being ignored by a parent who is staring at her phone can lead to "People aren't interested in what I have to say." After your business partner embezzles money, you might develop beliefs like "People can't be trusted" or "Business partnerships are dangerous."
- **Observations:** Watching other people go through experiences. If you watched your parents get cheated by a business partner, you might develop a belief that business partnership is dangerous or that entrepreneurship is an unstable or unreliable way to make a living. If you watched your dad making all the decisions in your family, you might conclude, "Men have all the power."
- **Hearing what others say:** Learning from religious institutions, school, parents, and other sources. If your single mom railed against men, you might develop a belief that all men are untrustworthy. From some sales training seminars, you might learn that sales is a slimy, manipulative process.

Remember our day trader, Tom, from Chapter 2? His self-doubts kept him from putting what he learned into practice. As a child, Tom was berated when he did things his father didn't like: "Why'd you do that? You should know better. You're such a disappointment." This happened repeatedly, leading Tom to conclude, "Mistakes and failures are bad" and "If I make a mistake or fail, I'll be rejected."

As an adult, these beliefs caused him to avoid taking chances, like moving to day trading, which in turn prevented him from becoming the entrepreneur he wanted to be. Tom was desperate to overcome his paralyzing fear of failure, but he couldn't do so until he eliminated the underlying belief that failure is bad, and that process started with identifying the source of his belief: his father's reaction when Tom did something his dad didn't like.

STEP 2: ALTERNATIVE INTERPRETATIONS

What are other ways of interpreting these events?

After you identify the source of your belief, the next step is to brainstorm alternative interpretations of the events that led to it.

Imagine you formed the belief "I'm an idiot." The source is your father calling you an idiot. You're watching a video of a scene from your childhood where your father says those words. Four other people are in the room, watching the video with you. After it plays, you turn to others and say, "See? I really am an idiot."

The others in the room, who didn't experience that moment as a child, each offer a different interpretation:

- "Your father thinks you're an idiot. It doesn't mean it's true."
- "Your father doesn't think you're an idiot. He had a habit of saying critical things to motivate you to do better."
- "Maybe you really *were* an idiot as a kid. Kids still have a lot to learn, but that doesn't mean you would *always* be an idiot."
- "Maybe he just said that because it's what he heard growing up—not because you are truly an idiot."

Each of these interpretations is valid and is nothing more than one way of looking at the events.

Take yourself out of the equation for a moment, and look at your own experience from an outsider's perspective. Ask yourself, "If I saw a dad calling his child an idiot, would I look at the kid and say, 'What an idiot!'?" Probably not. You might think the parent was stressed out and taking it out on their kid.

When the events happen to someone else, we can more easily see other ways of interpreting the events. And that's exactly what we need to do in this step.

STEP 3: NO SEEING

Did you really see your belief in the world?

Look around the room and pick an object. What color is it? What shape is it? Where is it located? Anything you can see has identifiable properties that anyone else who walks into the room will also be able to see. They will see the same color, shape, and location.

When you form a belief, it seems like you see it with the same clarity. But do you? Can you really see an abstraction? Can you see an idea of any kind? No. A video camera would only pick up the sights and sounds because that's all that's really there.

Another way to grasp this point is to imagine someone you know walks past you and doesn't say hi or acknowledge your presence. You might say to the person standing next to you, "See? I told you he doesn't like me!" In that situation, it seems like you can actually *see* that the person doesn't like you.

The truth is the person might have walked past you because he was distracted. Maybe he didn't see you. Maybe he is in a bad mood and doesn't want to talk to anyone. You don't really know.

So what did you see? Just someone walking by without saying hello.

The same is true of any abstract idea: you can't really see your belief in the world, only the events that led to your belief. A child can see she got an F; she cannot see "I'm stupid." A person can see that his business went belly up, but he can't see "I'll never succeed in business." Beliefs don't have a color, shape, or a location; events do.

So look at the events that happened to you. Doesn't it seem as if you saw your belief in the world, that you discovered your belief as if it were a fact?

Look again. Did you really see the belief? If you can see something, it will have color, size, and location. Like an apple. Color: red. Location: on the table. Size: fits in my hand. Did your belief have a color? Did it have a size? Did it have a location in the physical world?

No. You saw actions or heard words spoken, but you didn't actually see a belief even though it seems like you did.

If you didn't really see your belief, then what did you see that led to your belief? List the facts—the words and actions that everyone else could see too. You saw someone doing something. Or you noticed that something was absent. That's what happened.

Now, what if you have a belief that matches what people have said about you. For example, what if your belief is "There's something wrong with me," and the source of your belief is the fact that your parents really said, "There's something wrong with you"?

What do you do then?

You follow the same procedure. You note other ways of interpreting the events:

- That's what *they* think, but they could be wrong.
- Maybe *they* learned to speak that way to children from their parents but not because of your true characteristics.
- Maybe there was something wrong about your *behavior* but not you as a person.

Then look at the events again. Maybe you actually saw your parents say the words "There's something wrong with you," but did you really see the belief itself? Did you see that their words were the truth about you forever and always? No. You only heard what they said and how they said it.

If your belief was never out there in the world to be seen, where has it been all this time? The belief has only been in the mind.

If it makes sense that you didn't see the belief in the world, continue to the next step. If not, review the alternative interpretations you generated earlier. Imagine how you could have seen each of them in the source events. Then ask yourself, "Did I see a belief? Or did I see a series of events that had multiple interpretations? Can I see that the belief only existed in my mind, not in the world?"

STEP 4: NO MEANING

The source of the belief did happen. What meaning does it have? What do we know for sure because this happened?

After you identify the events that actually happened—what you actually saw and heard—the next step is to realize that those events have no inherent meaning. All meaning, that is, all *interpretation* of the events that happened, is in the mind—not in the events.

For example, if someone walks into a room and doesn't say hello, what might you possibly think?

- She doesn't like me.
- He is distracted.
- She is mad at me.

Or you might have come up with something else. All of these thoughts are meanings you attributed to the event. Where did those meanings come from? Your mind. All meaning comes from the mind.

The truth is we don't know anything for sure about ourselves, other people, or life as a result of the events.

Now hold on, you might think. *What happened to me was painful. It had consequences. I can't ignore them.* And you are right. Whatever happened did have consequences.

If you fail a subject in school, you may have to repeat the class, but that doesn't mean you're stupid or that you will never do well in that subject. If you say the "wrong" thing in a business meeting, the client may not like it, but that doesn't mean you are foolish. If you get fired, the consequence in the short term may be that you have to tighten your belt, but that doesn't mean you'll starve to death.

Consequences are real. But the meaning we give to those consequences is in our minds.

Think about the events at the source of your belief, and ask yourself, "Is there any meaning in those events that took place? Do I know anything for sure about myself, people, or life as a result of those events?"

STEP 5: KINESTHETIC/FEELING

If events have no meaning, can they make you feel anything?

Doesn't it seem like the events *made* you feel your belief? For example, if your belief is "I'm not good enough," then you feel not good enough because of what happened. If your belief is "Life is hard," then you feel like life is hard because of the events you experienced.

Consider this. Can events that have no meaning make you feel anything? If you walk down the street and a man walks by you, and that event has no meaning, what will you feel? Nothing. If you think the man is dangerous—in other words, if that's the meaning you give to this person's appearance—what will you feel? Fear. If you give his appearance the meaning "He'll protect me if something happens," what will you feel? Safe. It's the meaning you give events that produces your feelings, not the events themselves.

To make this more real, imagine that Aunt Shelly or Uncle Vahan were with you when you were forming your belief. They helped you see different interpretations of the events. Afterward, you decided on one of those alternative interpretations or meanings. Instead of concluding, "I'm not good enough" from your parents' criticism, you concluded, "Mom and Dad just don't have patience. That's why they react that way, not because of anything about me as a person." If you created this meaning, would you have felt not good enough? Wouldn't you have a very different feeling about the same events?

Imagine that someone wise whom you trust has helped you see another way of looking at the events. Imagine how it feels when you fully take in this new interpretation.

STEP 6: CHECK THE BELIEFS

Is the belief gone?

Now take a deep breath and say your old belief out loud.

Does it feel different? Does it feel flat or even silly? If not, go back to Step 3, "No Seeing." Make sure you really get that you couldn't see your belief in the events. Then go to Step 5 and make sure you really can feel a new feeling when you imagine the events with a new interpretation.

EXAMPLE: BRIAN ELIMINATES A BELIEF

Remember our example from Chapter 2 involving Brian? We left off at the point where Brian had discovered the belief that was limiting him: "I'm incompetent." Now let's see how he went through the Lefkoe Belief Elimination Process to get rid of that belief.

STEP 1: THE SOURCE

Facilitator: "What are the earliest experiences that may have led you to this belief 'I'm incompetent'?"

Brian: "I really don't know how I got that idea."

Facilitator: "Okay. It can be hard to figure out how we got a belief. One way to look at this is to think about how people important to you growing up reacted when you didn't get desired results. So how did they respond when that would happen?"

Brian: "My dad and my grandfather were just very critical people. So they'd criticize the shit out of me. They'd point out exactly what I'm doing, which is terrible because I already felt so terrible doing it. Everything I did wrong was picked apart and shoved in my face."

Facilitator: "Got it. Well, does it seem real to you that those events would lead you to conclude that I'm incompetent?"

Brian: "Yeah."

Facilitator: "Yeah. And can you see that it's not just you, but a lot of people who were your age who went through similar experiences might have formed a similar conclusion."

Brian: "Yeah."

STEP 2: ALTERNATIVE INTERPRETATIONS

Facilitator: "Next we want to find some other ways of looking at those events. So what else could it mean that your parents and grandfather would criticize you when you didn't get desired results?"

Brian: "Maybe that they thought criticism would make me learn my lesson from failing."

Facilitator: "Yeah, that's a great interpretation. What else could those events mean?"

Brian: "Maybe they didn't see a better way to teach me. So they used criticism."

Facilitator: "Right. That makes sense. What else?"

Brian: "I'm running out."

Facilitator: "Would you like me to suggest a few ideas?"

Brian: "Sure."

Facilitator: "One interpretation is you might not have been competent at the things they criticized you for at that time; that doesn't mean you would never learn to do those things."

Brian: "Ah, right."

Facilitator: "Another possibility is that even if you really were not competent at those things, does that mean you were fully incompetent at everything even then?"

Brian: "Definitely not. There were a lot of things I could do well."

Facilitator: "So we've come up with several ways to interpret those early experiences of getting criticism from your parents and grandfather. So is the belief you formed at the time "the truth" or just one of many ways of interpreting those events?"

Brian: "It's just one way."

STEP 3: NO SEEING

Facilitator: "But didn't it seem that at the time you formed the belief that you could see 'I'm incompetent'? That you discovered it like it was a fact?"

Brian: "Yes. It did seem [like I saw it]."

Facilitator: "For a moment let's take a look at what it really means to see something. Look around. You can see various objects in front of you. Notice each object has a color, a size, and a location."

Brian: "Uh-huh."

Facilitator: "And if someone else were to walk into the room and you pointed at the apple on the table, you'd know it was real because they would see the apple, be able to tell you its color and its location, right?"

Brian: "Right."

Facilitator: "When you form a belief, it seems like you could really see the belief in the world, that you discovered it. But look again.

Did you really see the belief [I'm incompetent] the way you can see an object with color, size and location?"

Brian: "No. I guess not. I just saw nothing."

Facilitator: "Well, you did see something. You saw how you were treated by your parents and grandfather."

Brian: "Yeah."

Facilitator: "And when you interpreted those events, that led you to your belief."

Brian: "Right."

Facilitator: "And can you see that the words they said to you and the way they reacted to you are specific, concrete events? That seeing those specific events is very different than seeing an abstraction like a belief?"

Brian: "Yeah, I get it now."

STEP 4: NO MEANING

Facilitator: "Now, when you were hearing the criticism that led to your belief, did you form the belief the very first time you heard the criticism or did it take repeated experiences?"

Brian: "Repeated experiences."

Facilitator: "That means there was a time when you were getting criticized when you hadn't formed the belief yet?"

Brian: "I guess so."

Facilitator: "After enough repeated experiences, you said, 'Aha, I know what this means.' So before you had that aha moment, what meaning did the events have?"

Brian: "Oh, I guess no meaning at all."

Facilitator: "And after you gave the events a meaning, where was the meaning? Was it out there in the world or someplace else?"

Brian: "Someplace else."

Facilitator: "Where was it?"

Brian: "In my mind."

Facilitator: "So can you see, then, that the events never carried any meaning. The meaning was just in the mind?"

Brian: "Yeah."

STEP 5: KINESTHETIC/FEELING

Facilitator: "To make this more real, imagine that when you were going through those experiences you met someone like me who helped you see other ways of interpreting the events. So you decided that when you were being criticized that it didn't mean you were not competent; instead, it must have meant they thought it was a good way to make sure you learned a lesson from those experiences. Really imagine those events happening and you're giving them that interpretation. How does that feel?"

Brian: "It feels pretty good. It feels freeing."

Facilitator: "So can you see that with a different interpretation, you would have felt differently?"

Brian: "Yes."

Facilitator: "Great. A lot of times the feelings we have seem like evidence that the belief is true. So when you felt not competent over and over it may have seemed like evidence that you really were not competent. But can you see that the feeling of not competent was caused by your interpretation of the events happening around you. So the feeling couldn't be evidence that the belief is true. Does that make sense?"

Brian: "Could you say that again?"

Facilitator: "Yeah, so when you were getting criticized by your grand-father and your parents, you interpreted that as 'I'm not competent.'"

Brian: "Right."

Facilitator: "As a result of that interpretation, you felt not competent."

Brian: "Okay."

Facilitator: "So the interpretation caused the feeling, and if that's true, then the feeling didn't prove anything about you."

Brian: "Yeah, right."

STEP 6: CHECK THE BELIEFS

Facilitator: "Great. So now let's check to see if we've made a change to this belief. Try saying 'I'm not competent' out loud again."

Brian: "I'm not competent."

Facilitator: "How does that feel?"

Brian: "It feels like nothing, really. Empty."

Facilitator: "And does it seem true at all?"

Brian: "No. Not at all. The words are just words now."

Facilitator: "Congratulations! You just got rid of a belief."

Brian: "Thanks."

Brian got rid of this belief by following the steps we've shown you in this chapter. Several weeks later, he reported that he was not so critical of his business partner and girlfriend. When you go through the belief process yourself, you may want to refer back to this example to guide you.

WORTH THE EFFORT

After reading about the six steps, you might be thinking, *Wow. It's going to take a lot of time and energy to eliminate just one belief!*

Remember the convicted felons from Chapter 1? Each one of them was able to eliminate at least one belief per session with Morty. That means it took them about sixty minutes to eliminate a belief that had been controlling their lives and leading them to unhealthy, unproductive actions for ten to twenty years. Not a bad return on investment.

Compare that to Vahan, who tried eliminating beliefs on his own without the benefit of the Lefkoe Belief Elimination Process. He was ultimately successful, but it took him several years to overcome the beliefs he had formed around money and selling himself and his business.

If you don't have the benefit of a facilitator like Brian did, it might take you a little longer to make the changes you want, but we're talking hours, not years. You have the steps. You've seen how eliminating beliefs can transform lives. You've got this!

We have many beliefs that can cause emotional reactions in the moment. If we get rid of the beliefs behind them, those reactions will stop. Sometimes, however, we don't have the time and energy to go through all six steps at the moment we're experiencing a negative feeling.

Good news! In the next chapter, we provide a process that neutralizes emotions in the moment without having to get rid of a belief first.

EXERCISE

Now it's your turn to eliminate a belief. Take a belief you found in the previous chapter or look at the list of thirty-five common beliefs in the appendix and pick one that you have. Then run through the six steps provided earlier:

1. The source

2. Alternating interpretations

3. No seeing

4. No meaning

5. Kinesthetic/feeling

6. Check the belief

Remember, if that seems too daunting, you can start by going to http://hittingthewall.net/, where you will find a video that can guide you through the steps for eliminating three common beliefs. That video will make the process described above come alive.

CHAPTER 4

ELIMINATING NEGATIVE FEELINGS IN MINUTES

In Stephen Covey's book *The 7 Habits of Highly Effective People*, Covey relates the following story:

> I was riding a subway on Sunday morning in New York. People were sitting quietly, reading papers, or resting with eyes closed. It was a peaceful scene. Then a man and his children entered the subway car. The man sat next to me and closed his eyes, apparently oblivious to his children, who were yelling, throwing things, even grabbing people's papers.

> I couldn't believe he could be so insensitive. Eventually, with what I felt was unusual patience, I turned and said, "Sir, your children are disturbing people. I wonder if you couldn't control them a little more?"

> The man lifted his gaze as if he saw the situation for the first time. "Oh, you're right," he said softly, "I guess I should do something about it. We just came from the hospital where their mother died

about an hour ago. I don't know what to think, and I guess they don't know how to handle it either."

Suddenly, I saw things differently. And because I saw differently, I felt differently. I behaved differently. My irritation vanished. I didn't have to worry about controlling my attitude or my behavior. My heart filled with compassion. "Your wife just died? Oh, I'm so sorry. Can you tell me about it? What can I do to help?"[3]

As soon as Covey gained a new perspective about the events on the subway, his emotional reaction changed. It was almost instantaneous, and the only thing that changed was the meaning he gave to the children's actions and the father's response.

This is perhaps an extreme example, but we all experience situations where we react to an event and experience negative emotions as a result:

- Someone cuts you off on the freeway
- A client does not retain you
- An investor pulls out of a deal
- Your spouse yells at you
- A longtime employee quits
- A friend doesn't return your call
- A colleague snubs you at work
- Your business loan application is denied

In each of these situations, what causes us to feel bad is how these events occur to us in the present moment, that is, the meaning we give to the event. For example:

---

3   Stephen R. Covey, *The 7 Habits of Highly Effective People* (New York: Simon & Schuster, 2020), 30–31.

- The person who cuts you off: *He's a jerk!*
- The longtime employee who quits: *We'll never find anyone that good again.*
- The investor who pulls out of the deal: *We're never going to get the funding we need.*
- The friend who doesn't call back: *She doesn't care about me.*
- The colleague who snubs you: *He thinks he's better than me.*

If these events occurred to you differently—for example, if you thought, *Wow. That driver must be in a hurry. I hope everything is okay*—you would have a completely different feeling about the same events. Instead of feeling upset, you would feel free to respond in more useful ways, just as Covey did.

Throughout this book we've made the point that beliefs cause recurring patterns of behaviors and emotions. Once we eliminate the belief, as described in Chapter 3, the behavioral and emotional patterns caused by that belief disappear. However, we won't always have the time to dig for a belief every time we have a bad feeling. So we need a way to deal with our reactions in the moment—a stopgap, so to speak, a way to dissolve the meaning we give to events—and thus stop the unwanted feeling in the moment.

That's where this chapter comes in. Using the Occurring Process can allow you to talk yourself through the situation, change your emotional response in the moment, and become more effective in how you handle life's varied circumstances.

THE LEFKOE OCCURRING PROCESS

Before we get into the process itself, let's clarify the difference between a belief and an occurring. A *belief*, such as any of the thirty-five listed in the appendix, has broad meaning that affects how we deal with people and life. As discussed in Chapter 2, it usually results from a series of events or experiences in the past, often as a child. An *occurring* is the meaning that occurs to you in the moment in response to one specific event. That meaning often comes from our beliefs, but it is not necessary to understand which belief in order to dissolve the emotional reaction in the moment.

An occurring fits this pattern:

- The client didn't renew our contract (event), which means our business is in trouble (occurring).
- Jessica ignored me today (event), which means she hates me (occurring).
- The gardener broke my garden gnome (event), which means he's careless (occurring).
- The client went with another provider (event), which means we can't get the big deals (occurring).
- An audience member fell asleep during my keynote presentation (event), which means I'm a boring public speaker (occurring).
- Adam didn't return my call after our last date (event), which means he's ghosting me and doesn't want to see me again (occurring).

The last example happened to Shelly. As a result of the meaning she gave the event, she felt disappointed and hurt. She later found out that Adam's favorite aunt had died and he had spent the week mourning and making funeral arrangements. If Shelly had followed the process we're going to share now, she could have spared herself a lot of frustration.

In short, the Lefkoe Occurring Process is a series of steps you can walk yourself through to change the meaning you give an event and therefore your emotional reaction. Fortunately, you don't need any special training to go through this process. It's something you can practice any time your occurrings cause you to feel stress, anxiety, or any negative feeling, that is, a feeling you don't want to have.

First we'll outline the six steps, and then we'll show you what it looks like to walk through the steps in several scenarios you might experience as an entrepreneur.

1. **Notice the feeling.** In other words, put a name to it. Are you feeling angry? Frustrated? Stressed? Anxious?
2. **Identify what happened right before the feeling (the event).** Describe the event in concrete terms without judgments or abstractions. For example, "A driver cut me off on the freeway," not "The jerk cut me off!" Your description should consist of what you can perceive with your five senses.
3. **Identify the meaning (occurring) you attributed to the event.** This is where the judgment comes in: "That driver's a jerk!" "She hates me." "He's ghosting me." You have to identify the meaning before you can change it.
4. **Create a few possible alternative interpretations.** Ask yourself, "What are other ways of explaining the same event? How might someone else see these circumstances?" Come up with two to three alternative interpretations. For example, the guy who cut you off might be rushing his pregnant wife to the hospital or hurrying to his son's all-star game.
5. **Realize that the meaning was in the mind, not in the events.** Abstractions and judgments—good, bad, mean, disrespectful, and so on—exist in our heads. They don't exist in the world.

Events have consequences, but they don't have inherent meaning. Interpretations only exist in our minds.

6. **Notice if the feeling is still there.** Look at the feeling you identified in Step 1. One of three things will have happened: (1) The feeling may be gone. (2) The feeling may be reduced. (3) The feeling may be gone, but another negative emotion may have come forward. If another negative emotion came up, you might try the process on other occurrings related to this event that you may not have noticed before. The more you use this process, the more you will find that the feeling is gone after you finish Step 5.

Let's say you are driving along a neighborhood street when another driver pulls out of their driveway right in front of you, causing you to nearly hit her car. You might feel anger and think, *Why didn't she look where she was going?* You're steaming for a while, but then you remember a book you read on how to better handle upsetting events like these.

1. **Notice the feeling. Anger.**
2. **Identify what happened right before the feeling.** Another driver pulled out in front of me, and I nearly hit her car.
3. **Identify the meaning you attributed to the event.** This driver is careless.
4. **Create a few possible alternative interpretations.**
   A. The driver was unable to turn her neck easily due to an unperceived condition.
   B. The driver was dealing with stressful news or an event that was distracting her.
   C. She was distracted by something at the time she was about to pull out of the driveway. For some reason, she did not notice me coming.

5. **Realize that the meaning was in the mind, not in the event.** The idea "This driver is careless" was in my mind, not in the world. I don't know anything about this person based on a single incident.
6. **Notice if the feeling is still there.** The feeling is gone. I'm not angry. In fact, I feel grateful that both of us were unharmed.

Situations like this happen every day, business related and not. As an entrepreneur, however, you have many opportunities to become anxious, stressed, and more. Remember our entrepreneur from the book's opening story? He could have used this process on a daily basis!

HOW ENTREPRENEURS USE THE OCCURRING PROCESS

In the following sections, we'll walk through a few examples step-by-step to help you understand how this process might be applied to different situations in your life as an entrepreneur.

THE FAILED PRODUCT LAUNCH

You just launched an online training course that you spent months designing. When you released it, the response was anticlimactic at best—the course was nearly empty.

1. **Notice the feeling.** Frustration.
2. **Identify what happened right before the feeling.** The number of registrations in my course was far lower than expected.
3. **Identify the meaning you attributed to the event.** I suck. I'm a failure. I'm going out of business.
4. **Create a few possible alternative interpretations.**

A. It wasn't my best product, but I learned a lot, so I can do better next time.

B. I didn't invest heavily enough in marketing, so there weren't enough eyes on it.

C. I can do more to increase my conversion rate, such as split testing. I can learn a lot from this.

5. **Realize that the meaning was in the mind, not in the event.** The low attendance doesn't mean I can't run a workshop. I don't know anything about myself because of that one event.

6. **Notice if the feeling is still there.** At first, I felt like the lack of registrations meant I was a failure, but now I see that I created that meaning. There are, in fact, other more productive meanings, so I no longer feel frustrated.

Everyone says that we should learn from our mistakes instead of fearing them. That's more easily said than done. But if you know how to let go of unhelpful meanings after a failure, you truly can profit whenever your strategies don't work, enabling you to succeed more in the future.

THE COMPETITION

During your most recent quarterly reports, you learn that your company is losing market share to the competition.

1. **Notice the feeling.** Urgency, panic, lack of control.

2. **Identify what happened right before the feeling.** Our competitor's market share has increased, and our market share has decreased by the same amount.

3. **Identify the meaning you attributed to the event.** We are going to be out of business! They've beaten us. I'm not sure we can recover.

4. **Create a few possible alternative interpretations.**
   A. Our strategy has not been as effective as their strategy so far, but that doesn't mean we won't learn from this and create a more effective approach in the future.
   B. We have great problem solvers on our team. Together we can come up with some new ideas.
   C. Once we figure out why they are beating us, we can use those insights to innovate an even better strategy than the one they are using.
5. **Realize that the meaning was in the mind, not in the event.** We don't know what the future will bring. But having let go of these negative meanings, we are now more likely to figure out how to succeed.
6. **Notice if the feeling is still there.** The feeling of panic subsided. I feel hopeful that we can figure out a way to win even though I don't have the answer yet.

Panicking often leads to short-term actions that can be destructive. But with hope for new possibilities, you are more likely to figure out how to equip your company for the future.

THE FURIOUS ADVISOR

You're a financial advisor managing a team of analysts. One day, you begin to have trouble with one of your analysts.

1. **Notice the feeling.** Fury.
2. **Identify what happened right before the feeling.** My analyst didn't follow a directive that I had given him.
3. **Identify the meaning you attributed to the event.** He's irresponsible. He doesn't respect me.
4. **Create a few possible alternative interpretations.**

A. Maybe I didn't communicate clearly.

B. Maybe there was a reason he didn't act on my directive that I don't yet know about.

5. **Realize that the meaning is in the mind, not in the event.** As a type A personality, I know I can respond to incidents like this with frustration. However, once I realized that I don't actually know what happened with my analyst, my anger went away.

6. **Notice if the feeling is still there.** I'm now calm about the situation. And since I don't know what happened, I'm merely curious.

Soon, you talk to the analyst and ask him what happened. It turns out that he had taken on an important client issue and was working tirelessly to mitigate the problem. Fortunately, because you eliminated your own meaning, you were not upset when you spoke to your analyst. You addressed his actions calmly and responsibly and quickly found a solution.

THE OVERWHELMED BUSINESS OWNER

Your business partner manages the day-to-day operations of your company. When he suddenly leaves, you become the de facto manager of those operations, in addition to your other responsibilities.

1. **Notice the feeling.** Panic, stress.

2. **Identify what happened right before the feeling.** During our weekly staff meeting, I looked at our income tracker and learned that we are tracking below our monthly goals.

3. **Identify the meaning you attributed to the event.** I'm not cut out to run a business.

4. **Create a few possible alternative interpretations.**

A. Maybe I'm lacking in some business skills now, but that doesn't mean I can't develop them over time.

B. Maybe this is a temporary downturn in our revenue, and with effort we can make up the shortfall.

5. **Realize that the meaning was in the mind, not in the event.** The idea that I am not cut out to run a business is in the mind. I can't draw any concrete conclusions about myself or my business acumen from the single fact that we are tracking below our monthly goals.

6. **Notice if the feeling is still there.** As soon as the meaning changed, my panic melted away.

Now that you are feeling more centered, you begin to address the issue productively with your team. "What's the best way to get that number up?" you ask. "Do we cut expenses? Double down on sales? Create a new product?" Instead of getting scared, you take action.

THE PRINTING BUSINESS

For decades, you and your thirty-five employees have run a four-color printing business that caters to the record industry. However, computer technology has changed the landscape.

1. **Notice the feeling.** Despair, uncertainty.

2. **Identify what happened right before the feeling.** The record industry is demanding our services in smaller and smaller quantities of late.

3. **Identify the meaning you attributed to the event.** I am going out of business. We are dinosaurs.

4. **Create a few possible alternative interpretations.**

A. My team still has strong design skills and decades of practical experience that can be applied in other areas.

B. We can start a whole new business.

5. **Realize that the meaning was in the mind, not in the event.** The change in the music industry created a real consequence: our service was no longer needed. But the idea that our business is doomed was only in the mind.

6. **Notice if the feeling is still there.** I don't feel despair anymore. Now I feel optimistic that we can find a way forward.

With this mindset shift, you recognize that the same forces that made your previous service obsolete also open up a need in the new digital environment. Soon, your business has gone from four-color printing to website design—and business is booming! (This printing example is the true story of Shelly's dear friend Letha Edwards, who started a web design business after she noticed demand in the four-color industry had been falling steeply as past clients had less and less need for those services. Her many competitors were not as nimble and shuttered in despair. She retired in 2021 after over twenty years running a successful web design business.)

HELPFUL HINTS

The more you try the exercise, the more quickly you will be able to apply it. If you practice daily, it will become an automatic response. As you are learning to use this process, it will be helpful to keep a few things in mind.

DON'T FRET ABOUT WHETHER YOUR ALTERNATIVE INTERPRETATIONS ARE "GOOD"

When applying Step 4, creating alternative interpretations of a given event, the purpose is to understand that other explanations are *possible*. That doesn't mean any one of them is the truth. The idea is to detach the event from the meaning you are giving it. Seeing that another meaning is possible demonstrates that meaning can't be inherent to the event. As such, whether those explanations are correct or not doesn't matter.

Let's use the failed product launch as an example. One alternative explanation was that you hadn't invested heavily enough in marketing. That's an opinion. Considering that idea, along with other options, can help you realize that your product launch's underwhelming performance does not prove "I am a failure" is *the* truth about you.

APPLY THE PROCESS APPROPRIATELY

In most cases, you will be taking yourself through this process. On the off chance you try to walk someone else through it, be wise in how you handle it. For instance, if a friend's partner recently passed on, it's not a good idea to approach them and say, "What meaning does their passing have? Can you see how the meaning is in your mind?"

Even when applying this process to your own emotional state, there are times when you may find it useful to let some time pass first. For example, if you've just had a terrible fight with a loved one, you may or may not be able to guide yourself through the Occurring Process. If you are, great. But if not, you may come back to it later to deal with some of the emotional fallout still in place.

FREE YOURSELF

The Lefkoe Occurring Process can be used in many different situations—anytime you have feelings after an unwanted experience.

One of Shelly's former clients used it to change the way she responded to an employee who tended to get frustrated and shut down during meetings. "He is rash and hard to deal with," Greta told Shelly.

After Greta saw that this was a meaning she gave to the employee's actions, her frustration dissolved. As a result, she was able to talk to him with an open mind.

After another meeting, Greta approached the employee and said, "I notice you seem to get frustrated sometimes during meetings. Is that true?"

He explained that sometimes he felt like people were unwilling to listen to his ideas about how to prevent problems—problems that he then had to solve later on. This insight allowed her to bring more critical discussion into their meetings, encouraging everyone to share their opinions and ideas about potential problems. As a result, she found that more great ideas were being voiced, and they were able to more quickly recognize the potential pitfalls of ideas they had quickly accepted in the past.

Vahan had just finished taking the Lefkoe Occurring Process course when he had the perfect opportunity to use what he had learned: he and his ex-wife were selling their house and putting their respective belongings into two different storage units in the same facility. When he discovered that his ex-wife's unit was toward the back of the facility, which was dark and foreboding at night, Vahan gave her the unit he was assigned, which was close to the entrance, and he took the one at the back.

Soon after, Vahan traveled to Europe for about a month. During that time, Vahan's ex-wife pulled her things out of storage and canceled her contract. Unfortunately, since they had switched units, that meant she inadvertently canceled the contract on the space where Vahan's belongings were stored. When the storage facility found the supposedly vacant unit full of belongings, they liquidated everything. Hundreds of thousands of dollars' worth of artwork, jewelry, coin collections, and photographs, as well as priceless items like childhood photos—gone.

When he discovered what had happened, Vahan was definitely shocked, but he didn't spiral into negative emotions. Because he had been using the Occurring Process already, he was able to talk himself through the situation.

He immediately asked himself, "What does this mean?"

"My stuff is gone. I wish it didn't happen. It really sucks. But it doesn't mean anything."

Because he wasn't stuck in negative feelings, Vahan was free to look at the possibilities in this situation: "Maybe I need to collect less stuff. Maybe I need to have more experiences instead."

Since then, Vahan has done just that. He has hiked Mount Kilimanjaro, built homes in the Nicaraguan jungle, and spent ten days in the African bush living with an ancient tribe. The

Occurring Process can set you free to live in a way you never dreamed of.

It can also be used to free yourself from emotional pain in the most devastating situations.

Shelly wanted to share this story in her own words:

> Losing Morty was the worst thing that ever happened to me. He was my best friend, partner in all things, father to my kids, and the love of my life. His death also had major consequences for the company we ran together and for my two daughters.
>
> Weeks after Morty died, I found myself not wanting to get out of bed. I'd spent weeks after his memorial grieving for him. Good, healthy grieving that honored our thirty-six-year marriage.
>
> But not being able to get out of bed was different from that grief. It was not healthy.
>
> How did I get through the worst of it? When waves of emotion would overpower me, I used the Occurring Process. It helped me see that his death, losing his presence in my day-to-day life, losing his business insight, losing him as the father of my children, did not mean my life was over. It did not mean my business would fail. It matters a *lot*. But it doesn't have any inherent meaning. The Occurring Process saved my life.

Here's how Shelly guided herself through the process during those especially difficult moments. First, she asked herself, "What happened that is making me not want to leave this bed?"

The answer was simple: "Morty died."

Then she asked herself, "Okay, what meaning am I giving that event?"

"It means I will starve to death because Morty was terrible with money and I have all this debt, and there is no way I can steer a company to success. I'm in trouble!"

She closed her eyes and rethought that last bit. Maybe Morty dying did mean she would starve to death. Or it could mean that she had the opportunity to gain financial acumen and lead this company to prosperity. So far, everything had always turned out for her in the end, even when the present looked bleak. And she had a network of loving, supportive people who would help her. She had everything in her favor. She could do this.

The truth was, Morty's death had no inherent meaning. It did not mean Shelly knew anything for sure about the future. His death just was. She could choose the meaning she gave it: that she was ruined *or* that she had an opportunity for change and to create a whole new second half. The power was hers.

That thought got her out of bed.

It was not that simple, though. The next day, Shelly had to do it all over again. This time, when she asked herself, "Okay, but what does it mean?" her brain told her "Morty dying means I will be alone forever."

She closed her eyes again and rethought. Maybe she would be

alone forever. Or maybe she would meet a fabulous, sexy entrepreneur and have a second act. She had a beautiful thirty-six-year marriage to learn from and be grateful for. She didn't have to give Morty's death a meaning that would strangle her life. It is a fact that he died, but the meaning she gave that event was in her control.

Morning after morning, Shelly chose the better, brighter meanings until there came a day when she didn't have to drag herself out of bed. Then, finally, a day when it wasn't a fight and she could actually create a good day. She did it by recognizing that it wasn't Morty's death that kept her in bed, but the meaning she gave to that event. And she could change that.

Today, Shelly is fully involved in creating her second act, as she calls it. She will always be grateful for what she had with Morty and honor who he was. His death no longer keeps her from living a full and joyful life.

Ultimately, that's what this process is all about: the freedom to get unstuck and explore possibilities that help propel you forward. Rather than being impacted by your circumstances, you can be free from the emotions and reactions that seemed so natural before. The process may take a while to master, but once you do, you begin to see possibilities in situations that you never would have seen before.

How exciting is that?

EXERCISE

The next time you find yourself upset, stressed, anxious, or filled with any other negative feeling, stop and walk yourself through the Lefkoe Occurring Process. We recommend writing down the steps at first, to guide yourself through the process. Over time, it will become more natural, and you likely won't need a written guide.

1. **Feeling:** Notice the feeling.

2. **Event:** Identify what happened right before the feeling.

3. **Occurring:** Identify the meaning you attributed to the event.

4. **Alternative interpretations:** Create a few possible alternative interpretations.

5. **Mind:** Realize that the meaning was in the mind, not in the events.

6. **Check:** Notice if the feeling is still there.

Morty used to guide people through a shortcut version of the process, which can be found in a TEDx Talk he gave in 2013 (https://www.youtube.com/watch?v=sMdVM-t5kFs& ab_channel=TEDxTalks) . The end result of the version presented in this chapter and the shortcut Morty used is the same: set yourself free from the emotion by understanding the meaning is in your mind, not the event. If you can do that, you'll be set free.

CHAPTER 5

SUCCESS ON YOUR OWN TERMS

As we have seen from the prior chapters of this book, most of the obstacles to achieving our goals are rooted in our beliefs. We've also seen how identifying and eliminating these beliefs can clear our path to success, both personally and professionally. But what is success? We're not talking about the definition from some book or business guru. What does success mean to *you*?

Some years ago, I (Vahan) was faced with this very question. I was running several companies, and on paper I was doing well, hitting all of the "success" markers—yet I did not feel successful. So I pursued more accolades, awards, and recognitions; I added more accomplishments and another degree to my résumé; and I spent more time working and pushing for increased growth and revenue in my companies—all for naught. Even as people congratulated me for receiving another award or reaching another benchmark, I wondered why I didn't feel like the successful person they saw.

It became clear that more of the same was not the solution. In search of answers, I looked inward and asked myself the important question every entrepreneur should be asking himself or herself: What does success look like *for me*? I realized that the success I had been chasing for years was success as defined by our society and culture. But was that also my own definition of success?

There was only one way to find out: I sat down and made a list of activities and experiences that made me feel successful. Earning recognition, receiving awards, launching more companies, making more money—none of these things were at the top of my list. Instead, I had things like spending quality time with my daughter, spending time with family and friends, taking my mom on trips, pursuing my passions (art, photography, exploring the world), physically challenging myself (running Spartan races, climbing mountains), doing charity work, and learning new skills.

Now I understood why I didn't feel successful. I had been focusing my efforts on the wrong things!

Of course, pursuing the items on my list meant spending time away from my companies, which meant hiring more staff to take care of tasks I had been doing so I could work away from the office.

And this is exactly what I have done. Thanks to my amazing team, I am now able to pursue the relationships and activities that make me feel successful. Of course, this comes at a financial cost, but my definition of success is not tied to how much money I make. Money is only a tool to attain the ultimate result: feeling successful and fulfilled by pursuing the things that truly matter to you.

Defining success is only the first step. To achieve that success, you need to identify and eliminate the beliefs and behavior patterns that have been holding you back. Doing so enables you to put down the heavy luggage you've been carrying around so you are free to perform better, faster, smarter, and in ways that are in line with what is most important to you.

EMPOWERING BELIEFS

After you let that baggage go, you're also free to adopt new beliefs that empower you to live and work in harmony with your deepest values. This is where you find meaning and purpose as an entrepreneur and as a human living on planet Earth. While these beliefs may vary from person to person, many seem to be quite universal.

Here are a few empowering beliefs I've adopted for myself:

- "Life is not happening *to* me. It is happening *for* me."
- "There is always a way to overcome a challenge."
- "I am responsible for the life I create."
- "Everything is always working out for me."

These types of beliefs have affected my thoughts, feelings, and actions in a positive and helpful way. They have allowed me to respond to challenges in a productive manner rather than react (or overreact) to them. They have allowed me to focus on solutions rather than problems and to see opportunities where others see limitations.

In February of 2022, I spoke to a group of business school graduates who expressed their frustration about the state of the economy and the high likelihood that a recession was coming our way. They saw this as a major problem and limitation to their ability to raise funds, launch their venture, and thrive as a new business.

I told them that while a recession does present many formidable challenges, it also offers some incredible opportunities. In fact, nearly half of the Fortune 500 companies were created during either a recession or a serious economic crisis. Here are just a few: Disney, HP, Hewlett-Packard, Hyatt Hotels, Microsoft, Trader Joe's, FedEx, Netflix, GE, and MTV. And then there are the companies that were launched during the major financial crisis of 2007–2009: Uber, Airbnb, Slack, Warby Parker, Venmo, Groupon, Instagram, Pinterest, Slack, Square, and more.

Most of the graduates didn't know these facts, and learning about these companies shifted their perspective from "Oh, I'm screwed if I try to start a business now" to "What opportunities do these challenging times present, especially for a new venture?"

You can make the same shift. During challenging times, whether due to economic crisis or market changes, you can focus on all of the problems and challenges, or you can look for opportunities in the market, as the founders of the above noted companies have.

This is just one example of how adopting an empowering belief like "There is always a way to overcome a challenge" can make all the difference. Once you've eliminated the beliefs holding you back, you can see all sorts of new possibilities. You just have to open the door and step out.

LIVING AND WORKING IN ALIGNMENT WITH YOUR VALUES

I think the ability to identify and eliminate beliefs is a superpower; it is a super powerful skill that gives us an advantage over those who carry limiting beliefs into their businesses and lives. It makes us almost bulletproof by giving us the ability to face and deal with challenges that are certain to come up in our entrepreneurial journey. What we do with this superpower is an important factor contributing to our feeling and achievement of success.

I strongly believe that solutions to the biggest problems humanity faces (environmental issues, food shortages, health crises, etc.) will not be coming from the government in Washington, DC, but rather from the world of conscious entrepreneurship.

Unlike politicians, who tend to be invested in the status quo with the main objective of being reelected, conscious entrepreneurs tend to challenge and question the status quo. They think outside the box and thrive in an environment of change and growth, constantly searching for better ways of doing things, for problems to solve, small or big. And the bigger the problem, the more valuable and profitable the solution.

At the same time, as entrepreneurs, we are often faced with the choice of compromising certain personal values for the company's "good." I was in that position several years ago when I was representing several high-net-worth individuals who were paying me handsomely to help them build and grow their companies, set up new ones, and invest in others. Very quickly their retainer became a sizable share of my revenue.

Simultaneously, however, I began to notice that their business practices and strategies were unscrupulous and at times unethical. After bringing this to their attention several times, I realized this was their modus operandi. Hence, I was faced with a choice: continue to collect large retainer checks while I watched them conduct business as usual or drop them and walk away from a big share of my company revenue.

While the choice was easy, the adjustment period was not, as my overhead and expenses stayed the same while my revenue decreased. But I knew that if this business relationship didn't align with my personal values, it didn't align with my company's values either. For better or worse, our businesses are a reflection of ourselves, who we are, what beliefs we hold, what we value. If I value integrity and honesty in my personal life, how can my company maintain relationships with clients who don't? Interestingly, within several months, as I concentrated on the clients who did align with my values and ethics, they began to grow and need me more. I also gained several new clients who more than made up for the drop caused by me walking away from those less ethical ones.

Knowing what you stand for creates a strong identity and brand that your customers will be drawn to and appreciate, at least those who share the same values. It also empowers you to say no to potential clients if the nature of their business goes against what you stand for. I've turned down a company that was in the cigarette business, another that sold sugary drinks for kids, one whose operation was polluting the environment, and one that was based on exploiting workers in a third-world country, all because their practices went against my values.

Something magical happens when you get your company aligned with your values, when you create and maintain a strong company identity, and when you communicate to the world what you stand for and don't waiver from that, even if it affects your bottom line. The tension between who you are personally and professionally disappears. You no longer have that inner struggle that comes along with compromising your values and justifying actions you know are wrong. You are able to be authentically you at home and at work, and your company will benefit as a result.

FOCUS ON VALUE

Over the years, my clients and I have looked for answers to various business questions: How do I increase my company revenue? How do I improve my client retention rate? How do I grow and scale my company?

What I have learned for myself and have seen time after time with my clients is that we have been asking questions that focus on the success of the business, which is important but not *the* thing to focus on. Albert Einstein once said, "Strive not to be a success, but rather to be of value."

Instead of only asking ourselves how to grow revenue and company reach, we should also be asking ourselves one simple question: "How do I deliver more value to my clients?" By serving our existing clients so that they experience more value, we see their businesses grow and blossom, which in turn creates more need for our services and enables us to grow with them.

In the last six years, I've witnessed this truth in action. My company has enjoyed robust growth rate, making it to *Inc.* magazine's Fastest-Growing Private Companies in the US the last five years in a row, as well as the *Financial Times'* list of Top 500 Fastest-

Growing Companies in the Americas, ahead of Amazon and Netflix.

It's not like we added a bunch of new clients over this period. Rather, we shifted our focus to taking better care of the clients we have. We started asking different questions focused on bringing more value to the client: How can I help my clients increase their revenue and grow? How can I better understand what my clients need and deliver it to them?

If you see the importance of focusing on the client but feel nervous about making this mindset shift, you might have some beliefs to identify and eliminate. Chapters 2 and 3 can help you there.

DOING GOOD

The old model used to be to build up your company and your revenue first, then give back and make a difference. The new model is to make a difference with the way you build up your company and revenue, and give back in the process.

Today's consumers care more than ever about who they buy from—about who you are as a brand and what you stand for. If doing good, giving back, and making a difference is not part of who you are as a company and how you do business, you are compromising your earning potential and leaving money on the table.

Years ago, I did pro bono cases for families seeking political asylum in the United States. One of the families I represented had a son who found me many years later and brought my law firm a very lucrative business deal. Another man became a client in an accident case because he remembered me from when I was in law school. He wasn't one of my professors; he was one of the janitors, and he remembered how I stopped to talk to him and ask about his family.

Doing good is not only the right thing to do; it's also good for business. It brings in and retains clients, and it also inspires and motivates your employees, who automatically become part of the cause and contributors toward it.

Though giving back has definitely helped our bottom line, it has had an even bigger impact on my life. When my company began its child sponsorship program many years ago, I had no idea how much I would get out of this simple, small gesture. Now we have two dozen sponsored kids, and I've taken trips to places like Cambodia, Guatemala, Nicaragua, Armenia, and Tanzania to build homes, schools, and wells; to support orphanages; and to help expose child sex trafficking and child labor rings. I can say with certainty that some of the most memorable moments, important lessons, and special connections made during these trips came from spending time with and getting to know the families and the children we are helping. I remember and cherish them far more than any award ceremony or business milestone celebration we have had in the last twenty-three years.

PASSION VERSUS PURPOSE

There has been a lot of talk about, as well as articles and books written about, finding and following one's true passion—almost like finding the "soulmate" version of a professional career.

When I was starting out as an attorney, the notion that I needed to find my passion made me question whether I was on the right path. I envied people who knew what they wanted to be from an early age and never even considered anything else.

My path was quite different: I went to art school and almost ended up in film school before going to law school, followed by business school. Even when I entered law school, my original plan was to get into diplomacy and international law, and then I finally found my way into business and corporate law.

While the road has been challenging at times, and I often questioned the path I had selected, I am grateful for this process, as it ultimately led me to find my purpose: helping, supporting, and protecting conscious entrepreneurs as they launch and grow their ventures, improving the world around us for this generation and many to come.

Like me, it took Shelly some time to find her purpose, but now she is equally passionate about what she's doing: helping people get rid of beliefs that hold them back. We both found our passion through finding our purpose. Finding our purpose, something bigger than ourselves, has given us a reason to push through challenges and difficult times. For me, this is more powerful than passion. As Pablo Picasso once said, "The meaning of life is to find your gift. The purpose of life is to give it away."

Have you found your purpose? If you've tried and haven't found it, beliefs may be in your way. You can have beliefs that keep you on a treadmill of activity with no time for the necessary reflection. You can even have beliefs that make you feel that finding your purpose is a bit too self-indulgent. To find your gift and then give it away, you need to be set free from the beliefs that hold you back.

WATER ALL OF THE PLANTS

When the Dalai Lama was asked what surprised him most about humanity, he answered "Man. Because he sacrifices his health in order to make money. Then he sacrifices money to recuperate his health. And then he is so anxious about the future that he does not enjoy the present."

As entrepreneurs, it's easy to be one of those who makes all kinds of sacrifices in an effort to build our business. Launching, operating, and growing a business is an enormous task that requires a huge commitment of time, energy, attention, and resources. The problem is that we can let it become such a priority that it trumps our own well-being: financial, physical, emotional, and mental.

While it is important and even necessary to give our business the attention and focus it requires to succeed, it behooves us not to do so to the detriment of our own well-being. After all, what's the point of having a successful business if you're not healthy enough to enjoy it or to use the fruits of your achievement to help others?

One of my former clients was an amazing entrepreneur who was "successfully" managing multiple ventures while also planning to acquire yet another business. During one of our meetings, I noticed that he did not look well and advised him to see a doctor.

"I'll do it after the deal closes," he replied. "I just don't have time right now."

When I saw him next, his condition had noticeably deteriorated. I gave him an ultimatum: go to the doctor or work on this deal stops. After his wife also insisted that he go see a doctor, he reluctantly complied. From the doctor's office, he was rushed straight to the hospital, and a few weeks later he perished.

Needless to say, he did not close the deal, and his other business ventures struggled without him. More importantly, he left behind a wife and two young kids. As Confucius once said, "A healthy man wants a thousand things. A sick man only wants one."

This tragic story has helped me keep the bigger picture in mind: my business is just one aspect of my life—one plant in my garden, so to speak. For my whole garden to thrive, I need to water all of the plants, not just the one called business. I need to give attention to my personal relationships, my health and fitness, my spirituality, my volunteering opportunities—all of the various aspects of my life. If my daughter is not thriving, then I'm not a success as a parent—or as an entrepreneur.

Watering doesn't just represent the time spent in a certain area. It's also a matter of awareness, understanding that there is more than one plant and that some plants need different kinds of attention. Mindfulness is the key, as is being proactive rather than reactive. Plan for how you're going to take care of all of the plants rather than reacting once you see something is going wrong.

Also consider this: if a business decision or long hours or difficult clients are costing you your health, peace of mind, relationships, or reputation, then it's too high a cost. The whole garden will suffer as a result.

HELL ON EARTH

Someone once defined hell as being your last day on Earth, when the person you became meets the person you could have become. I would add that it involves looking at the things you have done compared with what you could have done, the impact you could have had, the difference you could have made in people's lives, and the legacy you could have left.

I don't want to get to the end of my life without making a difference or reaching my full potential. Instead, I want to live a life that matters, a life worth living. This both drives me and gives me a purpose bigger than me and any of my business ventures. As entrepreneurs, we have a chance to create something special, something that will remain long after we are gone.

EXERCISE

This chapter is all about taking action so that you reach your full potential in every area of your life, not just your business endeavors.

Here's a to-do list to get you started:

1. Take a moment to write down the things that make you feel successful. What does your list look like? Is your definition of success aligned with your personal values? If it is not, you could be chasing someone else's definition of success and never truly feeling and experiencing success. Make a list and return to it every so often to update and upgrade it.

2. What is your purpose? What drives you in difficult times?

3. What will you leave behind? How do you want to be remembered? What would you like your legacy to be?

....

....

....

....

....

CONCLUSION

How do you want to be remembered?

Imagine you're at the funeral of someone you didn't know too well. Friends and family stand up and begin to say their goodbyes to this person they love. They wax eloquent about everything he did.

His best friend praises his popular TEDx Talk. His wife speaks proudly about his MBA from the University of Chicago. His eldest daughter lauds the successful company he built. His youngest child speaks admiringly about the three books he published. His brother-in-law praises his appearances on famous media, including the *Today* show.

Are you moved by what you hear? Touched?

It actually sounds a bit off, doesn't it? That's because it is. At your funeral, no one is going to talk about your fat bank account or your awards. These things don't matter to people; they're not what they remember.

The achievements listed above all belonged to Morty Lefkoe. When he died, a hundred people attended his funeral, fifty of whom stood up and shared why they loved this man—and not one talked about his achievements. People said he was the most loving man they'd known. Two people said they'd known him for forty years and he'd never said a bad word about anybody. Someone else talked about how he was always fully present with them, which made them feel special. Shelly's oldest daughter said how she not only knew she was loved every single day of her life, but she never, ever felt judged by her dad.

This was Morty—not his list of accomplishments.

As entrepreneurs, it's easy to think your achievements define you. But as Morty's funeral illustrates, they are not your legacy. Your legacy is how you affect the people in your life. The difference your being in their life made. Did you leave them empowered, better off than before, feeling loved or cared about? The success of your business is important; it's just not everything.

So many of us become entrepreneurs so that we can have freedom. Eliminating beliefs gives us that freedom.

The question is, how will you use this freedom?

GET ALIGNED WITH YOUR VALUES

Now that you have learned the lessons in this book, it's time to put the ideas into action. To become an empowered entrepreneur, you need to turn inward and put the same kind of work into yourself that you do into your business. This is a process of discovery. This is your chance to look at the person you *really* are, not the person your limiting beliefs have made you feel like you are.

Take some time to be quiet, to reflect and ask yourself some questions. If it helps you stay focused, write down your thoughts as you answer each one. The key is to look inside and be honest as you ask yourself.

- What is important to me? What are my values?
- What behaviors would I have to adopt to be more in alignment in my values? What behaviors would I have to stop?
- If nothing inside of me were holding me back, how would my life look different moving forward? How would it feel to have such a life?

In short, we want you to envision what life could be like if beliefs weren't holding you back—if all of the plants were watered and in full bloom, if every area of your life were vibrant and juicy.

If you do the work proposed in this book, that life and that legacy could be yours.

As you go on with your day, begin by being aware of unhelpful reactions you have or beliefs that emerge. Pay attention to your thoughts and the negative self-talk, the little voice that tries to remind you of your "limitations." As you work through this, be kind to yourself and acknowledge you're not perfect and you don't need to be.

Once you've identified an unhelpful belief, don't beat yourself up. Instead, seize the opportunity to learn and progress. The key, and often the hardest part, is to take that first step. If you can do that, you're on your way to creating a life that is in line with your values and where you feel empowered, successful, and fulfilled.

CREATE YOUR LEGACY

When you get to the end of your life, you don't want to look back and say, "Meh." You want to know that you lived a life worth living, one to be proud of, one that truly made a difference and brought joy to you and others. You want to know that you watered all of the plants and enjoyed the fullness of their vibrant bloom.

Eliminating beliefs can empower you to do so much more than become a successful entrepreneur, though it can and will do that too. Eliminating beliefs can empower you to

- Make wiser decisions
- Face and overcome challenges more effectively
- Better control your emotions
- Determine and focus on what matters most
- Take full responsibility for your life and your actions
- Be more open to embracing what life has to offer
- Be more present
- Establish and deepen connections
- Be and act more authentically
- Know and live your values

While many of these things may sound unrelated to building or running a successful business, they have everything to do with it. Your business is a reflection of you, and it will shine to the extent that you shine. Eliminating beliefs enables you to be the best version of yourself, constantly learning and improving yourself. This is how you build a business. This is how you reach your potential, professionally and personally.

How do you want to be remembered? Now is your chance to make yourself into that person. Identify the beliefs that are holding you back from fulfilling that vision, eliminate them, and step into the life you want.

EXERCISE

At birthday celebrations, Shelly and her family and friends participate in a ritual called What I Love about You. Each person takes a turn sharing what they love about the person celebrating a birthday. In all the years she has been leading this celebration, she has never once heard someone say, "What I love about you is how much money you have" or "What I love about you is how many awards you've won." Instead, they say things like "What I love about you is how warm and loving you are" and "What I love about you is the way you care for your spouse and kids."

What would happen if you tried this ritual with your friends and family? What would people say they love about you?

Now, what would you like people to say about you?

....

....

....

....

....

Are you living in a way that would lead people to say these things? If not, it's time to start.

APPENDIX

THIRTY-FIVE COMMON BELIEFS

Below is a list of thirty-five beliefs we've found as we helped thousands of people eliminate the beliefs that were limiting them. Read this list and notice which items strike a nerve. Say those that do out loud. You may notice that some of them produce a feeling that lets you know some part of you holds that belief. If so, use what you've learned in this book to eliminate that belief.

1. There's something wrong with me.
2. I'm not good enough.
3. I'm not capable.
4. I don't matter.
5. What I want doesn't matter.
6. What I feel doesn't matter.
7. What I do doesn't matter.
8. I'm not worthy.
9. I'm worthless.
10. I'm not okay.

11. I'm not important.
12. I'm not deserving.
13. I'm not lovable.
14. I'm powerless.
15. I'm stupid.
16. I'm bad.
17. I'm nothing.
18. Nothing I do is good enough.
19. I'm not attractive.
20. I'm ugly.
21. I'm not talented.
22. I'm weak.
23. I'm inadequate.
24. I'm not competent.
25. I'm a fake, a fraud, a phony.
26. I'm a disappointment.
27. I'm invisible.
28. I'm not acceptable.
29. I'm doomed.
30. I have nothing to offer.
31. My needs are not important.
32. I'm not trustworthy.
33. I'm a loser.
34. I'm defective.
35. I don't have what it takes.

ACKNOWLEDGMENTS

FROM SHELLY:

To Hilda and Jack, the best parents a human can have—I am grateful every day of my life for your love and guidance. Mom, I am who I am because of you.

To my incredible girls—thank you for being my North Stars. You inspire me every day. I am the luckiest mama in the world.

To Loki—thank you for bringing more love and joy into my life than I knew possible.

To Vahan—thank you for seeing the vision for this book and for being a shining star in my life. Thank you for modeling what a great dad really is and how you can be successful and still live a life worth living. I love and respect you more than you know.

To Rodney—thank you for all the years of dedication to making a difference in people's lives. Thank you for being there for me when Morty died. I don't know what I would have done without you. And thank you for all the help on this book. It is a better book because of you.

To Letha—thank you for fifty-five years of friendship. You are my person! Thank you for loving my husband and for being there for both of us always. Thank you for attending all the staff meetings. And for being the best godmother ever. You are my soul sister. I am grateful to my toes for your presence in my life.

To Lynda Brodsky—I can't imagine being on this planet without you. Thank you for always being there and for being my confidant and my rock for fifty-six years. Thanks for loving my girls. We are family.

To Marci Shimoff—thank you for reminding me that I could still have fun after Morty died and for being committed to making sure that happened. And it did. Thanks for being my fun friend and always, always being there. I love you.

To all of my friends who hold my hand and have my back on this journey through life—you mean everything to me. I wish I could name you all, but you know who you are.

To the Connecticut gang—I love you all.

A special thanks to my women's group, "The Women of Marin." You are my sisters. I am blessed beyond words to have you in my life.

To all of my clients—thank you for your courage to change and for trusting me. Helping people free themselves is what I get out of bed to do. It is a privilege.

To all the Lefkoe process facilitators—thank you for bringing this work out into the world with integrity.

To Amy—thank you for taking care of the books and caring about me and the company all of these years.

To Karen—thank you for your love and support and for running the show for all those years.

To Gail, our scribe—thank you for making this a better book. You were a joy to work with. You were patient and allowed us to go "off book" and laugh, which made the process so much easier and more fun! We love you.

To Meghan—thank you for hanging in there with us and seeing this to fruition.

FROM VAHAN:

To my family, my mom and dad, little monkey Ava, my sister and nieces, Mona and Mila, and to all my extended family—thank you for your unconditional love and support, and for always believing and encouraging me to be my best.

To my cousins TJ, Mika, Suro, and Anton—thank you for having my back and being there whenever I needed you.

To Art, my brother from another mother—thanks for your friendship and for constantly pushing me to do and be better. I appreciate you as a friend and as a business partner. You are a huge part of my success.

To Shelly—thank you for your friendship and all the laughs. Thank you for sharing your wisdom with me and the world. Your generous and loving spirit is an inspiration, and it has been an honor writing this book with you.

To my Gavaty group and friends—thank you for your friendship and for the amazing memories over the last two decades. Knowing that I can always count on every single one of you has been the biggest gift I could ever ask for.

To the Yepremyan Law Firm team—thank you for your dedication and tireless efforts to better serve our clients. I owe the success of our law firm all to you and your hard work.

To my clients—thank you for your trust in me and our law firm, and for the opportunity to serve you.

To Vishen—thank you for being a human connector. Without you and A-Fest, Shelly and I would have never met, and this book would have never been written. Thank you for inspiring me and setting an example of what conscious entrepreneurship looks like.

To Rodney—thank you for sharing your wisdom and time, and for helping us write this book. It is a much better book because of you and your valuable input.

To Gail and Meghan—thank you both for stepping in and walking us through the process of writing this book, and for your patience as we worked through finding our voice.

ABOUT THE AUTHORS

SHELLY LEFKOE is co-founder and CEO of the Lefkoe Institute. An international keynote speaker and workshop leader, Shelly has helped thousands of entrepreneurs rid themselves of limiting beliefs. Her programs have reached over 150,000 people worldwide. Her work has been featured on the *Today* show, *Leeza*, and many others.

VAHAN YEPREMYAN is a business attorney and founder of Yepremyan Law Firm, an award-winning and nationally recognized law firm. Vahan has helped thousands of entrepreneurs launch and scale their ventures. He holds a doctor of jurisprudence degree from the University of Southern California and a postgraduate diploma in entrepreneurship from Cambridge Judge Business School.

Printed in the USA
CPSIA information can be obtained
at www.ICGtesting.com
LVHW091039290923
759460LV00010B/133/J

9 781544 543703